PELHAM
HORSEMASTER SERIES

Judging Horses and Ponies

PELHAM HORSEMASTER SERIES

Judging Horses and Ponies

VALERIE RUSSELL

London
PELHAM BOOKS

First published in Great Britain by
PELHAM BOOKS LTD
52 Bedford Square
London WC1B 3EF
1978

ISBN 0 7207 1099 5

Photoset, printed and bound
in Great Britain by
REDWOOD BURN LIMITED
Trowbridge & Esher

CONTENTS

ILLUSTRATIONS

(between pages 86 and 87)

A fine Arab stallion showing all the qualities of the breed

A fine Welsh Cob (Section D) with a particularly attractive head

An Arab mare and her foal

Two-year-old Anglo-Arab colt

A splendid line-up of Shires

Clydesdale showing the strength and compactness of the breed

A pair of Suffolks

Fine Percheron showing the enormous strength of the breed

A good Quarter Horse stallion

Palomino going very kindly in harness

Well-marked Appaloosa yearling colt

A tandem going exceptionally well together

A good hackney

A well turned-out Western rider

Picture credits

All photographs by Leslie Lane, with the following exceptions: Percheron – by Monty

Palomino and Appaloosa – by the author

ACKNOWLEDGEMENTS

This book could not have been written without the help of the following judges, who gave so generously of their time and knowledge. When I first talked of writing it I was told by various people in the horse world that the idea was good, but: 'You'll *never, ever* get a judge to tell you what they look for.' Those people could not have been more wrong, and I would like to thank most sincerely the following judges, many of whom did not know me, nor I them, until I approached them for their help which they gave so willingly: Lady Miranda Emmett, Lady Violet Vernon, Lady D. M. Anderson, Hon. Mrs D. Rhys, Mrs J. Beaumont, Mrs D. Bourne, Mrs P. Brough, Mrs J. C. Compton, Mrs P. Howell, Mrs P. Lory, Mrs S. Mardon, Mrs S. McCosh, Mrs G. J. Mountain, Mrs G. F. S. Newall, Mrs E. Newbolt-Young, Mrs J. Ollivant, Mrs S. Parker, Mrs E. H. Parsons, Mrs J. Richardson, Mrs P. Stembridge, Mrs C. Westcott, Mrs D. S. D. Wort, Miss V. de Quincey, Miss O. Golby, Miss R. Kitching, Miss P. Linden, Miss M. Thompson, Miss P. Wood, R. Billington Esq., R. Claridge Esq., R. J. Clark Esq., M. Cox Esq., P. Dean Esq., I. V. Eckley Esq., A. T. Harley Esq., R. E. Hunt Esq., R. C. James Esq., J. M Johnston Esq., D. Keenleyside Esq., P. A. Lawson Esq., A. Pascoe Esq., J. Peate Esq., R. A. Peacock Esq., E. T. Sampson Esq., S. Watney Esq.

I would also like to thank J. F. Stephenson Esq. of the Cleveland Bay Horse Society for his help, and the following organisations which supplied me with information: The British Appaloosa Society, The British Show Hack and Cob Association, The British Show Pony Society, The Hunters' Improvement and Light Horse Breeding Society, the British Quarter Horse Association, The Western Horsemen's Association of Great Britain, The Shire Horse Society, The Suffolk Horse Society, The British Percheron Horse Society, The Hackney Horse Society.

INTRODUCTION

How often as a class leaves the ring at a horse show does one hear the question: 'What *are* the judges looking for?' expressed in tones that vary from exasperation to genuine enquiry? The same question is heard from spectators, some of whom are experienced exhibitors, and from those who just love horses and are trying to extend their knowledge of what is good and less good in each breed or type. The aim of this book is to provide at least some of the answers in a way that will enable readers to see horses and ponies through the eyes of the judges. As no one person could claim to be an expert judge of all classes and types, the information has been obtained by talking to judges in each category, with the object of presenting as wide a range of opinion as possible. Almost without exception the judges have stressed that judging is a matter of personal opinion, and indeed, if it were not, showing horses and ponies would lose that element of uncertainty which is at one and the same time fascinating and infuriating. Opinions can sometimes be very difficult to form, depending on the standard of animal presented. As one judge remarked, 'At big shows one is judging degrees of excellence; at smaller shows one is often judging degrees of mediocrity – it is debatable which presents the most problems.'

From the exhibitors' viewpoint, the judges offer one piece of advice: the only way to find out if an animal is suitable is to show it under a number of different judges. The wisdom of this was confirmed by the discussions on which this book is based. These showed quite clearly that while almost all judges are *looking* for much the same thing in their respective classes, the fact that results are so variable demonstrates that they actually *see* the points differently and attach different importance to them.

In general, only those classes that include the judging of conformation are discussed; those such as show-jumping, eventing, International Equestrian Federation combined driving, and dressage, which are marked almost entirely on performance around a set course or on a set series of movements, are felt to be outside the limits of this book.

As the book is written from the judges' viewpoint, little attempt is made to deal with the methods of schooling and presentation of horses in the ring. However, as nearly all judges emphasised the value of correct showing, mention is made from time to time of methods which either help or hinder their attempts to see each animal at its best.

At the risk of boring those with an encyclopaedic knowledge of horses and horsy terms, some endeavour has been made to define a number of apparently well-known terms. We all talk glibly of 'good, flat bone' and 'well-laid shoulder', but do we all know precisely what those terms mean? Similarly, some explanation of points of conformation has been included, together with some 'rule-of-thumb' methods of judging particular features, in the hope that they may be of help to those who are not fortunate enough to possess that invaluable asset: 'a natural eye for a horse'.

The chapter on hunters has been used as the main vehicle for detailed explanations, but most of the points discussed there apply equally to other types and breeds.

With a few exceptions, Championship judging has been omitted, chiefly because it would involve tedious repetition of subjects previously discussed. However, the judges did make a few observations about Championships in general that are well worth mentioning. They pointed out that apparent anomalies, such as a horse coming only second in its class being chosen as Supreme Champion, are not necessarily as contradictory as they may at first seem. The Championship *must* be judged on the way the animals are presented in that class *and no other*. The eventual Champion may have gone less well in its earlier class, or the other animals may have become tired or soured during the course of the day. Alternatively, a Championship is often judged by a panel, who just may not agree with the original assessment. There was also some disagreement among judges about the type of animal that should win a Championship. Some felt that a gelding, because of its lack of breeding potential, should be awarded a major Championship only in exceptional circumstances. Others put forward the view that in a Supreme Championship, a ridden pony should be the logical winner in preference to in-hand exhibits. They supported their opinions by pointing out that horses and ponies are bred primarily to be ridden, and that the ridden animal is the ultimate proof of success or failure. They contended that a brood mare might never produce another foal, that young stock may not develop satisfactorily, and that, with few exceptions, it is not possible in the show-ring to judge the true worth of a stallion as a sire. Needless to say, there is another body of opinion totally opposed to those views, and who maintain that the *best* animal must win.

3

Judges of all breeds come in for a great deal of criticism from exhibitors and spectators alike, for a variety of real or imagined transgressions. No one – least of all the judges themselves – pretends that he or she is perfect, and some are obviously much better and much more impartial than others, but it would be difficult to point to any activity where this is not the case. However, in the course of compiling this book, during which I had the pleasure of talking to dozens of judges, it became clear that the majority are not only deeply conscious of their responsibilities, but also deeply appreciative of what they regard as the great privilege of being asked to judge other people's animals. All agreed that they expected criticism, and most are fully prepared to give to owners and exhibitors (but not to casual enquirers) some indication of their reasons for the placing given to a particular animal. Some even make a point of walking around the lines or boxes afterwards for that very purpose.

Finally, a timely word from a very experienced judge to all exhibitors: 'At the end of the show you have the same animal as you had at the beginning. It is no better for having been first or worse for being last.'

Chapter 1

HUNTERS AND GENERAL INFORMATION ABOUT JUDGING

The Ridden Hunter classes at the leading shows are contested by top-class animals of the type that any keen hunting man or woman would long to ride to hounds. Although many of the winning horses are probably far too valuable to risk in the hurly-burly of the hunting field, they nevertheless occupy an important place in the horse world, setting a standard of near perfection towards which breeders should aim.

When a class of Ridden Hunters enters the ring, the judge's first impressions are vitally important, because, as several judges remarked, 'First impressions are very often lasting impressions.' This is particularly so in a hunter class, where most judges tend to sort the horses very quickly into those giving the overall impression of having the strength, endurance, conformation and common sense to give them a comfortable, enjoyable and safe ride during a day's hunting, and those which, for a variety of reasons, do not. It does not mean, of course, that the judge is attempting to place the class in its final order as the animals walk round the ring for the first time. However, it does indicate that during this vital stage, a reasonably accurate opinion can be formed of which animals are going to be called in

5

near the top of the line and which are going to be 'also-rans'.

The individual features most likely to attract attention in the early stages are a generally pleasing outline, a free, long-striding walk, manners, quality, and presence. To present an attractive outline, a horse needs to carry its head well, with the nose just a little in front of the vertical, the neck slightly arched, and the hocks moving well under the body. An animal that pokes its nose and looks 'strung out' does not provoke a favourable initial reaction.

In a hunter, as indeed in any horse or pony, the walk is important, not only for its own sake, but also because it gives a remarkably accurate indication of what the animal's other paces will be. The judge looks for a full, effortless stride, with the movement of the forelegs originating from the shoulders and not from the knees, and with the hindlegs coming well under the body, ensuring that the imprints of the hindfeet overreach those of the forefeet.

The need for good manners in a hunter is obvious, and an animal that enters the ring fighting for its head, jiggling from side to side or showing any form of disobedience, is unlikely to find favour, no matter how good its conformation. A horse that really misbehaves, particularly to the extent of rearing, will probably be asked to leave the ring.

'Presence' and 'quality' are two words that crop up again and again when describing top-class horses, and both are difficult to define as they cannot be explained wholly in terms of physical attributes. Most people would agree that presence is the ability possessed by some horses to *compel* the judge (and others) to look at them and be drawn to look again, almost involuntarily. In human terms the nearest parallel is probably that star quality which sets a great

6

actor or actress apart from the merely very good. A rather apt description of a show horse with presence is one that 'comes into the ring with the air of knowing, absolutely, that it is in the right place, at the right time, and [in a ridden class] wearing the right rider.' It has more to do with character, personality and great pride of bearing than with conformation as such. It certainly has nothing to do with size. A Shetland can have as much presence as a Shire, and it is just as evident when the animal is turned out in the field as when it is presented in the show-ring. It is an invaluable asset, and some judges, when confronted with one horse having almost perfect conformation, but little or no presence, and another of slightly less good conformation but enormous presence, will prefer the latter.

Quality, too, is frequently referred to as 'that indefinable attribute'; few can say exactly what they mean by it, yet none are in any doubt that they can recognise it immediately. A consensus of opinion suggests that it is an exceptional degree of excellence, elegance, good breeding, and fineness (as distinct from coarseness) of appearance. Quality is most obvious in the head, with emphasis on the delicate sculpting of the bones, and the fine etching of the blood-vessels through the soft, silky skin. Individual animals of every breed and type may show quality, although it is perhaps less obvious in the heavier breeds.

When the judge has gained initial impressions of each horse, the class trots on. At this pace, a hunter should move forward freely with a long, level stride, the toes well pointed without being flicked forward, and the movement, as always, coming from the shoulder. While knee action should be kept to a minimum, some judges do not like a real 'daisy-cutter' (an animal with very low action), as they consider it unsuitable and even unsafe over the rough

7

country likely to be encountered out hunting. Behind, the hocks must be well flexed and brought right under the body. Extravagant action in front, but with the hindlegs 'left behind', as sometimes seen, is not favoured. At the canter, the judge notes particularly those horses that appear to be giving their riders a smooth, comfortable ride, and are able to produce generous extension when asked, while maintaining a balanced, rhythmic movement. A mental note will almost certainly be made of horses that appear to have difficulty in striking off on the correct leg at the canter; this is so the judge can decide, during his ride, whether this was due to the stiffness of the horse or to a less than skilful rider.

The gallop is obviously an important pace in a hunter, with preference given to a horse that moves fast and freely with a long, raking stride. A good length of stride is particularly significant in hunters as it means that the periods of relaxation *between* strides are longer, thus muscle fatigue is likely to be less than in a shorter-striding animal. A bad fault is appearing to 'gallop into the ground', i.e. a horse that has so much knee action that it gives the impression of pounding up and down almost on the spot instead of moving forward freely and effortlessly.

Most ridden classes go round the ring on the right rein first, and are later asked to change the rein across the ring, with the judge noting, once more, any horse that has difficulty striking off on the correct leg. After showing their paces on the left rein, the class is called into line more or less in the anticipated final order. In a very large class, and if time is short, those with such obvious faults of conformation, type, or action as to disqualify them from the final placings, may reluctantly be asked to retire at this stage.

Next comes the judge's ride, a vitally important part of

showing and many a class is won or lost as a result of it. A clever exhibitor can, as everyone knows, make a horse appear a much better ride than it really is, and a less skilled one can fail to bring out the best in a good horse. Any doubts in the judge's mind are likely to be resolved when he rides the horse himself.

As a top-class show hunter must have perfect manners, it will be expected to stand like a rock while the judge mounts and to remain stationary until given the order to move forward. During the ride, the judge looks for ready response to the aids, smooth and comfortable transitions up *and* down, correct striking off at the canter, and a horse that is happy in its mouth, with no head throwing or shaking. When asked to gallop on, it should extend smoothly and willingly, giving the feeling that it can maintain the faster pace without undue effort. Few judges mind if the horse 'takes hold' a bit at the canter and the gallop, and indeed most, especially men, believe that a hunter should do so to show it has boldness and courage, but it *must* pull up easily without fighting the bit or in any way becoming over-excited. On the other hand, a horse that 'folds up' in front as soon as the rider takes a feel on the reins is almost universally disliked. All in all, the judge looks for a comfortable, well-balanced, light-mouthed ride from a well-schooled, sensible horse that responds to the lightest of aids and leaves the judge with the feeling that *this* is the one he or she would choose to ride for a day's hunting.

The judge's ride over, the horses are stripped of their saddles and examined individually. Methods for this vary from judge to judge. Some, aware of the adage 'no foot, no 'oss', start their examination at the feet; others prefer to begin at the head, assessing much of the horse's character from its eyes and general outlook. But whichever method is used, the aim is the same: to look carefully at each point of conformation; to note any unacceptable lumps and bumps that show up only under close scrutiny; to make sure the animal stands square; to see that it moves straight and true; and to compare one with another in detail.

For the purpose of describing the points of conformation, it seems logical to start at the head. In a top-class hunter this should be lean and reasonably small, but in proportion to the rest of the body, especially to the length of the neck. An excessively small head not only imparts an undesirable pony appearance to the horse, but almost certainly does not allow adequate bone surface for the attachment of the muscles concerned with chewing, free movement of the head, and the movement of the front legs. A large head is unsightly and alters the whole balance of the animal, making it unacceptably heavy on the hands. Good width between the ears is sought, with the head tapering to a fine muzzle, free of any coarse hair that would indicate common blood. The judge looks for large, sensitive, flexible nostrils, as these, together with the wide windpipe this type of nostril usually indicates, are essential for the free flow of air to the lungs – an absolute necessity in a hunter that is required to maintain fast paces over long distances.

If the eyes of man are 'a mirror of the soul', most horse judges would consider the eyes of the horse to be a mirror of its temperament and character. Large, but not too prominent eyes are required in a hunter. They should be set wide apart and high on the head, with an intelligent, generous, kindly, yet bold expression. Opinion varies a little about a horse that shows the whites of the eyes; some judges believe it denotes an evil temper and few really like it because it looks unattractive. However, a horse with a big eye socket is bound to show white all round the eye, but this has no bearing on temperament, and is unlikely to be penalised if the other features are good.

The judge looks for ears of reasonable size — certainly not so small as to give a pony look — and they should be well-pricked, mobile, and covered with fine, thin skin and hair.

It is unlikely that a horse with an over- or under-shot jaw would be presented at a large show, but these malformations can and do appear at smaller shows and are considered a very serious fault. A good, strong jawline is essential, with ample room for the respiratory tract between the two sides of the jawbone at the neck end. There must also be plenty of space between the posterior edges of the jawbone and the neck to allow freedom of the parotid gland when the horse is flexing its head and neck. Any compression of this gland causes discomfort and inevitably leads to evasions. The judge expects to see a nicely curved junction between the neck and jaw, not a sharp angle that would constrict the windpipe.

In any riding-horse, the neck is extremely important, not only because it is used by the animal as a means of balancing, but also because it and the head are the parts of the horse constantly seen by the rider and their formation can play a significant role in the giving or otherwise of confidence in the animal as a ride. A very short neck, especially if accompanied by a short, straight shoulder, gives the rider the insecure feeling that he has nothing in front of him, and an over-long neck, which is usually thin and weedy as well, gives the rider the impression that the reins are attached to a mobile and at times uncontrollable piece of india-rubber.

The neck is one of the parts of the body to which various terms are applied, the meaning and significance of which are not always fully appreciated. A hunter judge looks for an animal with a neck that tapers gradually towards its upper end and is moderately long and thin compared with those of other types and breeds where speed is not an important factor. This is because the length of the neck also indicates the length of the muscle attached to the top of the neck at one end and the middle of the humerus (the lower of the two bones making up the shoulder), at the other, which is chiefly responsible for pulling the forelimbs forward. It follows that a good (but not exaggerated) length of neck, and thus of this particular muscle, will favour generous extension of the forelimbs, giving the long stride that covers the ground with minimum effort. However, the neck must have sufficient depth and substance to be in proportion to the rest of the body. Apart from the feeling of insecurity engendered in the rider, an unduly long, thin neck lacks the strength to hold the head up efficiently, while a very short, muscular one is often inflexible and indicates a puller.

The upper line of the neck, from where it dips just in front of the withers to where it joins the head, should make a graceful curve; the lower line should always slope upwards and outwards from the chest. A judge will penalise any marked convexity of the lower line. This denotes either incorrect schooling leading to over-development of the muscles and resultant faulty head-carriage, or, when accompanied by concavity of the upper line of the neck, what is known as a 'ewe' neck, which is not only unsightly, but usually results in the horse carrying its head too high with its nose poked out. Equally, no judge will be impressed with a swan-necked horse, i.e. one with a pronounced convexity of the upper third of the neck, combined with an almost vertical set of the head. The judge looks for a neck that contributes to a 'good length of rein', and to do this, it must be longer on its upper than on its under side. This also enables the neck to be arched correctly and the head to be set at the correct angle – that is, with the nose slightly in advance of the vertical when the horse is standing at rest but interested.

Moving to the shoulders, all judges agree that a well-laid, sloping shoulder is essential, together with suitably formed withers. 'A good length of rein' in a hunter must come from a well-laid shoulder and moderate length of neck, and not from a long neck and indifferent shoulder. Less experienced exhibitors and spectators sometimes have difficulty in judging the slope of the shoulder, and its relation to the withers, so a brief explanation may be helpful.

The shoulder is often spoken of as if it consisted of one bone only, but in reality it is made up of two – the broad, flat shoulder-blade or scapula which runs diagonally forward from just below the withers and articulates with the second element of the shoulder, the upper arm bone or humerus. This in turn articulates with the bones of the forearm at its other end.

The centre of the joint formed by the articulation of shoulder-blade and humerus is known as the point of the shoulder, and is covered with tendon and muscle. It can be seen and felt just slightly below and behind where the base of the neck merges into the chest, and it is the line from this point to the top of the shoulder-blade which ends just under the withers, that gives the slope of the shoulder. In a hunter, a judge expects to see a shoulder sloping at approximately 55 degrees from the vertical. A wide shoulder-blade with adequate room for attachment of the muscles that control the movement of the forelimb is essential. Length of shoulder-blade is also sought in a hunter because the longer and more sloping it is, the more scope there is for free forward movement of the humerus, thus giving the desired long stride. Heavy, bunchy muscling of the shoulder, especially around the point, is known as a 'loaded' shoulder and is considered a fault in a riding-horse, as it restricts movement.

The withers, formed by the spiny processes of the vertebrae which are more developed in this area than in the remainder of the spine, should be well formed, as it is to these bones that many of the muscles, ligaments and tendons concerned in the movement of the forelegs are attached. They should also run well back, as they provide the area of attachment of the shoulder-blade, and any deficiency in this respect inevitably leads to a narrow, upright shoulder. Hunter judges do not favour either very high or very low withers. The former do not stand continuous hard work, and often, when combined with a high shoulder-blade, tend to produce unacceptably high knee action. They also present problems with the fitting of the saddle. Low withers, as well as allowing the saddle to slip forward, are often found in horses that have rather upright shoulders, and, as previously mentioned, their lack of size restricts muscle attachment. Moderately narrow withers are preferred in riding-horses – the rather wide, coarse ones sometimes found in heavyweight hunters are considered a fault.

Anatomically, the withers are not part of the shoulder, and although experienced judges are unlikely to be misled, some less experienced observers may take them into account when assessing the slope of the shoulder, and this can lead to errors. It is quite possible for an animal to have fine, high withers, and at the same time a straight, narrow shoulder – a combination no competent hunter judge would accept.

The forearm will come in for close scrutiny, and in a horse such as a hunter, where speed is important, this

14

should be long, allowing for long, strong muscles. The elbow joint, formed by the articulation of the humerus and the forearm, must not be set too close to the body ('tied in') as this restricts the freedom of movement of the leg. It must neither turn in, as this makes the horse throw its foreleg outwards and gives an unpleasant rolling movement, nor turn outwards, as this causes the toes to turn in and, apart from the resultant poor action, it is often the cause of corns and even splints, because of the uneven pressure on the inside of the foot, and the consequent uneven distribution of weight on the leg.

The judge will examine the knee joint carefully from all angles. From the front, this joint should be large, wide and flat, offering a good surface area for the muscles, ligaments and tendons. From the side, it must look perpendicular, with no bony protruberances, and no forward or backward deviation (known respectively as 'over' and 'back' at the knee). If obliged to choose, judges prefer an animal that is slightly over, as this rarely causes unsoundness, whereas a horse that is back at the knee is universally disliked because of the excessive strain this puts on the tendons and ligaments of the lower leg. From behind, the knee should look small and will only appear so if the trapezium bone at the back of the knee is large – again offering a good attachment area.

Great importance is attached by the judge to the leg between the knee and the fetlock – and this is another point of the horse's conformation about which there is some misunderstanding. It is here that the 'bone' of the horse is measured, and it is sometimes implied that this measurement consists of bone only. In fact it consists of the cannon-bone, the two sesamoid- or splint-bones that lie on either side of the cannon-bone, *and* the associated tendons, ligaments

15

and fibrous tissue. In a lightweight hunter the judges expect at least 8 inches of bone (measured just below the knee) and in a heavyweight a minimum of 9 inches. They look not only at the actual amount of bone, but at the general quality, shape, and length of the lower leg. It should be short and straight, and the associated ligaments and tendons must be as near parallel as possible with the cannon. These should feel hard to the touch, with no sign of softness or roundness. A judge looks for 'flat' bone, which means that the cannon, when viewed from the side, should be absolutely straight with an almost flat surface and boldly defined tendons and ligaments. Seen from the front, the cannon must show a clean outline from knee to fetlock. 'Round' bone is a serious fault. This has, as the name suggests, a rounded, puffy appearance when viewed from any angle, and the tendons are neither prominent nor clearly outlined. Some horses are 'tied in' below the knee, i.e. when the measurement of the cannon immediately below the knee is smaller than it is further down. This is a bad fault in conformation.

The fetlock joint should be broad and flattened on all sides, with roundness being considered a fault. Hunter judges like to see a moderately long, sloping pastern, but excess of either slope or length, while giving a comfortable ride, is a weakness and will be treated accordingly. Short, upright pasterns are a defect, as they cannot act as efficient shock absorbers and are often found in horses with upright shoulders.

The judge will look carefully at the feet, making sure that both forefeet are the same size and shape, reasonably broad, and neither too small nor too large for the size of the horse. Small, upright, boxy-looking feet are greatly disliked, as are feet with a low, narrow heel. The angle of the

16

toe with the ground should be approximately 45 – 50 degrees when viewed from the side, and should be parallel with the long pastern bone. There is rarely time for the judge to pick up the feet of all the entries, but if he does, a surfeit of hoof oil will not be appreciated! All judges note if the horn looks healthy, and any signs of shelliness or of sandcracks are unlikely to be missed.

Having examined the front end of the horse in detail, some judges stand back and view the animal first from the side and then from the front. Consciously in some instances, and almost unconsciously in others, they are weighing up the overall shape and proportions of the front. From the side, a vertical line dropped from the point of the shoulder should meet the ground nearly at the point of the toe. If the foot is in front of the line when the horse is standing squarely, the leg is set forward at a slight angle and this limits action; if the leg below the knee inclines forward, this indicates a calf-kneed animal. If the feet are behind the vertical line, the legs will then be too far under the horse, making for heaviness in hand and a tendency to stumble because too much body weight is thrown onto the leg.

Also from the side, a vertical line from the middle of the forearm should equally divide the knee, cannon and pastern, reaching the ground just behind the heel. If the line falls within the heel, the pasterns are probably too upright, and if it falls a considerable distance behind, the pasterns will have too great a slope.

From the front, a vertical line from the middle of the forearm should equally divide all the structures below, i.e. the knee, fetlock joint, and foot. If the line tends to the outer side of these, the legs are too close together ('coming out of the same hole'), while if it passes through the inner side, the legs are too far apart. These two deviations also indicate that the chest is too narrow or too wide in front respectively.

Because of the necessity for endurance and sustained speed in a hunter, the judge looks for a horse with a deep, long chest, allowing plenty of room for expansion of the lungs. Generally speaking, it is easy to see if a horse is lacking in depth, but in a well-proportioned, mature animal the judge looks for one that measures approximately the same from withers to breastbone as from breastbone to the centre of the pastern. The ribs should be long, and when seen from the front, give an oval, not rounded, shape to the body. A very flat-sided horse will be penalised. From the side, the ribs should slope backwards. A judge does not want to see too much space between the last rib and the point of the hip (a hand's breadth is an average measurement in a hunter, as distinct from a pony). Too much space causes slackness of the loins, which contributes to a weak, often over-long back. Sometimes the last ribs are short and insufficiently arched – a fault known as 'light in the ribs', in contrast to being 'well ribbed-up'.

A hunter judge looks for a horse with a strong, muscular back that is neither too long (normally indicating lack of staying power), nor too short (and consequently lacking flexibility). Some accept a *slightly* longer back as being preferable to a very short one because the former is usually accompanied by a long chest with its ample lung room. A longer back, however, must be very well muscled. In outline, the back should be almost level and should certainly not have a pronounced dip, or show any sign of convexity (roach-backed).

The loins must be short, well-muscled and wide. Some judges like to see almost horizontal loins; others prefer

18

those that slope slightly upwards from the rear of the last rib to the croup. No judge likes to see long, slack loins, as this constitutes a weakness, but due allowance is usually made for the little extra length normally seen in mares, although this must not be pronounced.

The croup of the hunter should be slightly convex in outline, well rounded, and with plenty of muscle. A sloping croup giving rise to a 'goose-rump' although often taken to indicate jumping ability, has no place in the show hunter. The quarters must be well developed and covered by strong, firm muscle. A well-set tail, i.e. one set high and almost in line with the spine, completes an attractive top line. Coarse or wavy hair in the tail is taken as a sign of common blood. The judge will also note, when walking round the horse, whether the hip-bones are level when the horse is standing squarely – as, of course, it should be for the judge's inspection. It is not unknown for a judge to lift a horse's tail unexpectedly to see if there is a momentary resistance, indicating general stamina and strength. It also gives the judge the opportunity to see if the animal is too 'split up behind'.

The hindleg of the hunter is examined closely, as it is from here that the propulsive power of the horse comes. The judge looks for a well-developed, muscular thigh and second thigh, and a strong stifle with no signs of puffiness or weakness. Particular attention is paid to the hock, which must have a clean, clearly defined outline, with a large, wide, flat surface for muscle attachment and for the absorption of concussion. When viewed from the side, the hock must be wide both above and below the joint, and a line dropped from the seat bone to the point of the hock should be vertical. Although some judges insist that the straighter the hock the better, others disagree, maintaining that a very straight hock, especially if combined with a short leg, does not allow sufficient extension to give adequate propulsion at the faster paces. The latter group of judges also point to the fact that hocks which are situated well in front of a vertical line from the seat bone are more liable to lead to a slipping of the stifle. Hocks that fall *behind* the vertical line from the seat bone are equally undesirable, while sickle hocks (those which show an exaggerated curve of the line leading to the joint) are very much disliked, particularly as this results in the cannonbone sloping forward to a marked degree in many instances. This in turn can lead to overreaching. From behind, the judge checks that a vertical line from the point of the hock divides the limb below it equally. Hocks which turn out (wide behind) or turn in (cow-hocks) are defects in themselves; they usually lead in the former case to the feet turning inwards, and in the latter to the feet turning out. All these factors lead to poor action and will not find favour. Some horses are either too wide or too narrow right from the hip-bone. This leads to the hocks being too wide or too close together, although it does not necessarily follow that the hocks will turn in or out.

The phrase 'well let-down hocks' is used frequently with regard to all riding-horses and ponies, and is perhaps one of the most misunderstood of horsy terms. Judges know exactly what they mean by it, but a few comments may be of interest. The phrase implies that the hock is as near the ground as possible, and this in turn suggests the shortest possible cannon-bone. However, some judges (and vets) believe that this is to some extent an optical illusion, and also, a matter of relative proportions. Taking the illusory aspect first, a horse with sickle hocks will almost certainly appear less well let-down because the more bent formation leads the eye upwards from the point of the hock rather than downwards. An animal with very sloping pasterns will tend to look well let-down because, irrespective of the length of the cannon, the hocks will actually be nearer the ground than in an animal with straighter pasterns. When it comes to proportions, a rule-of-thumb check is to measure mentally the distance from the fold of the stifle across to the point of the hock, and from the point of the hock to the ground. These distances should be equal, or very nearly so. Thus, when the judge looks at the hocks, the associated structures are also taken into account before a final decision is reached.

Having summed up the quality of the leg, the judge examines the hindfeet, expecting them to be as sound and well shaped as the forefeet, although they are normally slightly more upright and a little narrower.

The detailed examination completed, the judge will probably stand back and have another look at the animal as a whole, making a final check of its general shape and proportions. There are various ways of actually measuring to see if a horse is of good proportions, and although most judges possess a good enough eye to be able to tell just by looking at the animal, a mention of one of the simplest methods may be of help to prospective exhibitors and to spectators alike.

In a well-proportioned riding-horse the length of the head from poll to muzzle should be equal to: the distance from the chestnut to the ground on the foreleg; the depth of the body at the lowest part of the back; the fold of the stifle to the croup; the point of the hock to the fold of the stifle; the point of the hock to the ground; the posterior angle of the shoulder-blade to the haunch-bone. From the point of the shoulder to the seat-bone should be about two and a half times the length of the head.

In addition, the height from the fetlock to the elbow should be equal to the height from elbow to wither, and the distances from seat-bone to haunch-bone, from seat-bone to stifle, and from stifle to haunch-bone should all be approximately equal to each other, but not equal to the length of the head. Generally speaking, a riding-horse whose height is much greater than its length will be 'leggy', while if the reverse is true, the back will almost certainly be too long. (These proportions are a combination of those appearing in *Horses in Action* by R. H. Smythe, and *Points of the Horse* by Capt. M. Horace Hayes, who in turn acknowledge other sources.)

This, then, is the basic conformation for which judges are looking in Ridden Hunter classes, and with some variations, in most classes of riding-horses. These variations will be mentioned as they arise.

Next, the judge asks the individual exhibitor to walk the horse away and trot it back past him. In a ridden class, this is solely for the judge to see that the animal moves correctly and straight at the walk and the trot, and does not dish (throw the forelegs outwards in a circular movement) or plait (swing the legs inwards so that they appear almost to cross) or perhaps drop one hip. The judge also notes if the animal goes too close or too wide in front or behind – suspicion of this will have been aroused by previous inspection of conformation, and in the case of going too close, by any signs of brushing on the inside of the legs. Judges do not like an animal that goes too wide, but if faced with a choice, prefer this to the potential danger of a horse that goes too close and is thus liable to fall over its own feet.

Judges of all ridden classes have remarked on the common fault of competitors who trot their animals too fast and on a tight rein at this stage, in a misguided effort to impress with their horse's ability to produce spectacular action and cover the ground. All this is likely to do is accentuate any fault. As one judge commented, 'This is not what we look for at this stage in a ridden class. We've already seen the animal's paces and assessed them during our ride. We're looking for straightness of movement, as up till now we've probably seen the action in profile only.' Judges are, not unnaturally, suspicious of exhibitors who run their horses out in anything but a straight line, as this is often an attempt to disguise faulty action by not allowing the judge a direct view of it. Some judges even assume that there *is* something wrong with the action if a horse is presented in this way, and may place it down the line, as they have not been able to see it properly.

With this final stage of judging completed, the class is sent out again in a small circle so that the judge may have a last look and perhaps adjust the placings in his mind before calling them into line in the final order. Most judges agree that if, at this point, they have been confronted with two horses that are almost inseparable on conformation, ride and action, they will choose the one they would most like to ride for a day's hunting. This is so much a matter of personal preference and almost of instinctive choice by individual judges that it is virtually impossible to indicate any one feature that is certain to tip the balance in favour of a particular horse. Some judges always prefer the horse with the best front; others the one with the best hindleg, and so on. Colour, too, can be influential. Few judges are impressed by wishy-washy colour, and are likely to prefer a good strong bay, brown, or grey, with not too much white.

At the larger shows in Britain, the hunter classes are nearly all affiliated to the Hunters' Improvement and National Light Horse Breeding Society, and are judged under the Society's rules by one, and sometimes two members of the Society's Judges' Panel. Ridden Show Hunter classes, which are open to mares and geldings, are usually divided into separate classes according to their weight-carrying ability and not according to height. Entries for the lightweight classes must be capable of carrying up to 13 stone; the middleweights of carrying 13 stone and not more than 14 stone 7lb; and the heavyweights of carrying over 14 stone 7lb. If there are only two classes, these will be for lightweights capable of carrying 13 stone 7lb and under, and heavyweights capable of carrying over 13 stone 7lb. If, as sometimes happens, a judge believes that a horse is up to more weight than the class in which it is entered, he may transfer it to the higher weight class. The only Ridden Hunter class in which entry is restricted as to size is the Small Hunter, which must be 15.2 hands or under.

Ladies' Hunter classes are frequently included, and these are for animals suitable for and to be ridden by a lady side-saddle. There are no height or weight restrictions placed on entries, but they tend to be of the light to middleweight type of animal. In classes for Novice Ridden Hunters, no restrictions as to height and weight are imposed, but entries must not have won a first prize of value £15 or over in any Ridden Hunter, Working Hunter, Hack or Cob class, either in Britain or abroad before the closing date of entries for the show in question. (The £15 limit applied at the time of publication in 1978.)

Working Hunters may be divided into two classes – one for horses capable of carrying 13 stone 7lb and under, and the other for those capable of carrying over that weight.

In general, all animals shown in the ridden classes must

be four years old or more.

From the foregoing, it can be seen that judges may be confronted with a variety of classes at any one show, and although they look for the same basic conformation, action and ride in all, brief mention should be made of special features to be taken into account in individual classes.

For instance, in the lightweight class, particularly at some of the smaller shows, the entries may include horses that are of good conformation, have excellent action, give a lovely ride, but are not of true hunter type. They possibly have too little bone and substance for a genuine hunter, and a bit too much refinement, suggesting that they would be more suitable in a Hack class. If the class also includes some genuine hunter-types that are as good as, or superior in conformation, action, and ride to the hack-type, no problem arises. However, if the hack-type is, in the judge's view, the best animal in the class *except* for type, then a decision must be made as to whether to put up the hack, or to put up a hunter-type with some fairly obvious fault in conformation or action. There are no hard and fast rules governing this situation, and the final placings will vary from judge to judge. This illustration is included more to demonstrate the dilemma judges can be faced with than to state exactly how they will judge the class. It may, however, help exhibitors and spectators to appreciate why a good animal somewhat lacking in type is placed below an inferior animal of undoubted type, or vice versa.

In the middle- and heavyweight classes, the judges do not expect to get quite the same light and airy ride as in the lightweight class, although if they do, it is very much in the animal's favour. In the heavyweight class especially, judges are conscious of one or two conformation faults that are more prevalent than in the lighter divisions. Weight-carrying horses sometimes have a tendency to overall coarseness, and in particular their withers may be rather broad. Both are possibly a legacy from some heavy-horse blood in their background. The other far from rare fault is a heavy body on legs that are lacking in bone and look spindly. Such a 'heavy-topped' horse does not find favour with a hunter judge.

In Small Hunter classes the judge looks for an animal with substance and bone, and probably one that can carry more weight than a lightweight of comparable height. It is not a class in which the judge's requirements are easily determined. Some say they look for 'something a little more cobby' than a lightweight, and then correct themselves, realising that this is not *precisely* what they mean. Generally, however, they look for a small, compact horse that is up to some weight, and are more or less agreed that they do not like the 'light, airy-fairy, hack-type animal'.

In Novice classes (usually for four-year-olds), the judge makes some allowance for a little youthful exuberance and may not be quite so strict about manners as in the classes for mature animals. A certain greenness of performance, with the young horse not yet quite able to produce the finished paces and polished ride of the older animals, is accepted. However, basic faults in action and conformation are no more acceptable in a novice than in a mature animal. Although in all other ridden classes, the judges come to their decisions about the various animals as they have been presented to them on that day, in a Novice class some consideration is given to whether the youngster looks like developing into a good hunter at maturity.

Ladies' Hunters, which are ridden side-saddle, must, in addition to being true hunter-types, have absolutely impeccable manners and smooth, unexaggerated paces. Further details of the requirements of the ideal side-saddle mount are included in the chapter on hacks and cobs.

Working Hunter classes affiliated to the Hunters' Improvement Society (and most others as well) are judged in two separate sections. First the entries must jump a course of not less than six natural-looking fences with a maximum height of 3 ft 9 in., and following this they are judged on conformation, action, ride, etc. as in an ordinary Ridden Hunter class. Forty per cent of the marks are allotted to the jumping phase, of which 30 per cent are for the actual jumping, and 10 per cent for style; the remaining 60 per cent of marks are allocated to the show section.

Although the show section is judged exactly as in a Ridden Hunter class, the standard of the entry, particularly at some smaller shows, is often lower, and the judges tend to place more emphasis on the 'working' ability of the horse than on sheer good looks. For example, most judges will not penalise a working hunter for the occasional scar or blemish which clearly does not affect its way of going, whereas in a Ridden Hunter show class (which is much more of a beauty contest) this would be taken into account in nearly all cases. Nevertheless, if two horses in a Working Hunter class were virtually equal in every other way, the blemish-free animal would take the honours.

In the jumping phase, the judge looks for a horse that goes on smoothly at a fair hunting pace and takes the fences neatly and calmly. The jumping style sometimes seen in the show-jumping arena, with the horse being 'hooked back' in front of fences, is not favoured by working-hunter judges. Refusals are very heavily penalised, with most judges saying that no matter how good the horse's make and shape, a stop in the jumping phase should put it right down the line. There is *some* divergence of opinion over this, but not much. Ideally, the horse should jump the fence clear, but if a knock-down is involved, the judge is likely to be harsher on the horse that takes the obstacle by the roots than on the one that just tips a rail with his hindfeet. However, this is left to the judge's discretion.

Under Hunters' Improvement Society rules, competitors are not permitted to change the horse's tack between phases – a point the conscientious judge will bear in mind.

HUNTER BREEDING CLASSES

BROOD MARES

In addition to looking for basic points of conformation, which are just as important in a brood mare as in any other horse – perhaps even more so, as bad points may be passed on to succeeding generations – the judge likes to see a big, roomy, feminine-looking mare with quality, and a kindly, generous outlook. The judge also looks for a little more length of back than would be acceptable in a male, for plenty of room between the pelvic bones, and for a reasonably long line underneath. All these features ensure room for carrying a foal. Allowances are usually made for a slightly dipped back, especially in an older mare, and injury scars will almost certainly be ignored. Some judges look at the mare's teats to see if they are adequate.

The judge likes to see a mare that looks as if she has the attributes of a 'good mum'. This is rather a vague and sometimes misleading point, especially if the mare does not have a foal at foot. Even if she has, there is some division of opinion on whether the mare's attitude to her foal in the show-ring should be taken into account, as the conditions are so far from natural.

When walked and trotted up, the judge will look for

28

straight and true action, but *may* be lenient with lameness obviously caused by accident. Allowance is certainly made for the fact that the mare's action is likely to be less free and brisk than an animal that is in work, as the muscle tone is bound to be different. In addition, some of the mares will be older than the entries in the average ridden class, and years of bearing foals clearly affects their way of going.

YOUNG STOCK

Almost without exception, judges agree that foal classes are by far the most difficult to assess, principally because of the enormous differences even a week of age can make. They feel that the older foals usually have an unfair advantage, and some judges try to overcome this by estimating how each individual foal is going to mature. Others believe that this allows too much room for error, and that in any event, the foals should be judged on the day. Some look at the dam, and note which features the foal has in common with her, and whether it is *perhaps* going to develop into something similar. Of all classes, this is the one in which there is the greatest variation in the judges' approach and opinions.

There is nevertheless some common ground. All look for straight limbs, a well-laid shoulder, and a nicely shaped head. Most agree that it is possible to see if the youngster is going to have sufficient bone, or whether it has spindly, match-stick-like legs that are never likely to improve. As everyone knows, it is difficult to persuade a very young foal to walk or trot for the judge, and even if it does, it is probable that the hocks of the youngest ones may almost touch behind through sheer infantile lack of strength, and no judge is likely to pay much attention to this. The youngest also tend to be a little straight in the pasterns, and although this will probably alter with age, it just may not. A glance to see if the shoulder is also straight may persuade the judge that the pasterns are unlikely to improve greatly with maturity. All in all, judges acknowledge that they are rarely entirely happy with their decisions in foal classes, and point out that they may place a foal near the bottom of the line one week and near the top just a week or so later. This is not necessarily inconsistency – it merely reflects the rapid changes that can take place in foals in a very short time.

Judging other young stock, such as yearlings and two- and three-year-olds, also presents problems, but the general feeling is that these are not quite so difficult as foals. Once again, conformation must be good, but the judge obviously makes allowance for lack of development in the neck for instance, and to some extent, behind the saddle. Yearlings especially look rather leggy, and this most judges take into account, emphasising that so long as the rest of the body is more or less in proportion it is not necessarily serious. Youngsters that appear to have a *great deal* of daylight under them, however, are not liked by hunter judges, as their chances of maturing into animals of any substance are not very great. This feature is more serious in two- and three-year-olds, as most hunter types should have out-grown real legginess by this stage. Some yearlings and two-year-olds tend to go either too close or too wide behind; the judge looks more leniently on the former of these, believing that it will probably improve with age whereas the young-ster that goes wide behind is less likely to improve. Judges bear in mind that colts tend to mature more slowly than fillies.

A point often overlooked is that in youngsters, the muscles along the back should be level with or higher than the vertebral processes of the spine.

There is marked disagreement among judges (of all

breeds and types) about youngsters that show signs of normal, youthful, uneven growth, and have croups markedly higher than the withers. Some judges say they are quite happy to take this into account and make allowance for it, although they would be inclined to favour an animal that happened to be even on the day, if it came to a close decision. Others state quite categorically that they believe youngsters going through this stage should be left at home until they have evened up. Only by trial and error can exhibitors learn which judges hold which views.

Manners in young-stock classes are taken less into account than in classes of mature animals, although judges make the point (which should be obvious to exhibitors) that if a youngster behaves so badly that it is impossible to see it properly, it will be at a great disadvantage. Vicious or dangerous behaviour is, of course, another thing again, and in *any* class an animal behaving in such a manner will be asked to leave the ring.

CLEVELAND BAYS

Although in the past, Cleveland Bays were well known as carriage-horses, today they are chiefly (but not exclusively) used for crossing with Thoroughbreds to produce hunters with substance and quality. They are therefore included in this section on hunter breeding stock, and in the show-ring most Cleveland Bay judges assess the horses from this point of view, although some still take into account the features required in a carriage-horse.

As a class enters the ring, the judges look first for type and the more obvious breed characteristics. They expect to see big, powerful, deep-bodied horses, with relatively short legs which should have at least 9 inches of good-quality bone. A mare should be a minimum of 16 hands; a stallion may be over 17 hands, but the average is about 16.2. The head is typically rather large — certainly bigger than a Thoroughbred of comparable size — but it should not be coarse or common-looking. As the name implies, Clevelands are typically bay in colour, with black legs, mane, and tail. Legs that are red or bay below the knee are considered a fault, but not so serious as to disqualify a horse altogether. The manes and tails are normally profuse, but the tails are sometimes pulled on show animals — a practice greatly disliked by some judges.

As the class moves round the ring, the judges look for a free-moving, long-striding animal, with the action originating from the shoulder. When the trot is considered, there is a measure of disagreement among the judges. Some look for a degree of knee action — more than in a good Thoroughbred, for instance; others like the action to be as near daisy-cutting as possible. All, however, look for good flexion of the hocks. A direct quotation from the official *Cleveland Bay Standard of Points for Judges* states: 'High action is not characteristic of the breed. The Cleveland which moves well and which is full of courage will move freely from the shoulder and will flex his knees and hocks sufficiently. The action required is free all round, gets over the ground, and fits the wear and tear qualities of the breed.' Cleveland Bays are renowned for their trotting ability, and it used to be said that a Cleveland should walk five miles in the hour and trot fifteen. In the show-ring the walk can be seen but the really fast trot has, as one judge put it, 'to be taken on trust'. In the old days, Cleveland stallions were shown by men wearing plimsolls who entered the ring running at top speed and trotted the animals round, and even then the horses were not fully extended!

Having absorbed first impressions, the judge lines the

class up for the individual inspection. Starting at the head, he will look for an animal with a bold but kindly expression in large, well-set eyes. Roman noses are not encouraged in the breed, but it is unlikely that a horse would be placed right down the line for that fault alone. The ears should be quite large, but fine, and the head as a whole must be well set on to a typically rather long, lean neck. In some strains of Clevelands, grey hairs are found in the mane (and the tail) and this is acceptable, but any white, other than a small star, is not.

The shoulders must be sloping, deep, and well-muscled without being loaded. Earlier generations of Clevelands were inclined to be rather long in the back, but today, judges are looking for something shorter, with strong, muscular loins. Some have a tendency to slack loins, and this the judges penalise. The quarters must be strong, of good length, oval in outline, and almost level, with the tail well set-up. As already stated, a deep body, with plenty of heart room and a good spring of rib, is a breed characteristic.

A muscular forearm, large knees, and good flat bone are as important in Clevelands as in any other breed, and perhaps even more so, as they are often cross-bred with the lighter, poorer type of Thoroughbred to which they should impart more bone and overall substance. The legs are free of superfluous hair. The pasterns should be sloping, but not too long, and great store is set by good feet, with hard, blue horn. Shallow or narrow feet are uncommon; in general, the breed has excellent feet, and any departure from this high standard will be severely penalised.

Muscular thighs and second thighs are essential, as are good, clean hocks. Special attention will be paid to the hindleg, if only because, once again, the type of Thoroughbred with which Clevelands are often crossed are sometimes deficient in this respect. With this in mind at least one judge, if obliged to choose between a Cleveland with bad hocks and one which was a bit short in front, would give preference to the latter. Judges who regard the breed more as carriage-horses disagree, and go for the animal with the better front. A slightly longer back and legs are also favoured for carriage work.

Although the Breed Standard mentions 16–16.2 hands as being the range of heights for Clevelands, it also states that 'height should not disqualify an otherwise good sort'. Judges, of course, have their own preferences. Some like a big horse of 17 hands or more, which looks magnificent provided it has retained its type, but it must be said that these are the ones that are inclined to longer backs and lightness in the loins. Others suggest that in a breed primarily used for crossing, great size may be acceptable when put to a smallish Thoroughbred, but might present problems if crossed with a large one.

Throughout the class, the judges will have noted each horse's character and temperament. Clevelands are usually sensible and although possessing strong characters which can be spoilt by weak handling (a trait not confined to this breed!) they are characteristically honest and bold.

After the individual inspection, each horse is walked and trotted out so that the judge may check for the essential straight, true, and level action. Any deviation from this – especially the tendency to dish found in some Clevelands – is considered a serious defect.

As Cleveland Bays are not regarded primarily as riding-horses, they are always shown in-hand and not under saddle.

Chapter 2

HACKS AND COBS

HACKS

A well-known judge, having seen the word 'hack' defined in the Oxford Dictionary as 'a hired horse' or 'an ordinary horse' commented with some feeling, 'Far may *that* be from the show hack of today!' And indeed, the modern first-class show hack should be anything but ordinary, combining as it does the very highest standards of conformation, action, and manners to produce a riding-horse that is as near perfection as possible.

Classes for these lovely animals are, at the larger shows at least, affiliated to the British Show Hack and Cob Association and are judged according to the Association's rules by members of the Panel of Recommended Judges. Two classes are normally included: one for Small Hacks, open to mares and geldings exceeding 14.2 hands but not exceeding 15 hands; the other for Large Hacks, open to mares and geldings exceeding 15 hands but not exceeding 15.3. If only one class is held, this should cover the full height range. There may also be separate classes for Novice Hacks that have not won a total of £25 or more in hack classes, Ladies' and Pairs classes excepted, at shows affiliated to the Association, at the closing date; and for Ladies'

Hacks, open to mares and geldings exceeding 14.2 hands and not exceeding 15.3, suitable to carry and to be ridden by a lady side-saddle.

The Association has laid down a scheme of marking to be adopted by its judges, allocating 40 per cent of the marks for conformation, presence, type, and action in-hand, and 60 per cent for ride, training test, and manners.

When a hack class enters the ring, the judge looks first for outstanding elegance and quality, for great presence and for true hack type. The latter is hard to describe, but most judges seek the ultimate in a beautiful riding-horse, with a refined head that is neither too large nor (especially in the Small Hack class) of pony type; an exceptional front; a perfectly proportioned body of a rather lighter frame than a hunter, yet with no hint of weediness; altogether an animal that carries itself proudly, and moves with out-standing grace and lightness of foot.

A significant contribution to the overall picture of extreme refinement is made by the turn-out of both horse and rider. A poorly turned-out horse – no matter how good its conformation – is not going to attract the judge's attention as quickly as another whose coat gleams with well-being, and whose mane and tail are beautifully plaited. The turn-out of the rider is perhaps more important in hack classes than in any other, as no horse can look really elegant with an unkempt rider on top.

As the class proceeds round the ring on the right rein, the judge looks for horses with a fluent, well-balanced walk, and when they trot on, a light, almost gliding pace is sought, with toes well pointed, and plenty of impulsion. A smooth transition from the trot into a graceful, free, elastic and comfortable-looking canter is sought, and at all paces the head must be in the correct position – neither over-bent, nor with the nose poking forward.

Good manners are mandatory in a hack, and any tendency towards disobedience, over-exuberance or sourness will be penalised rigorously. Nappiness or rearing will almost certainly result in the competitor being asked to retire from the class. Age, of course, is taken into account when considering training and manners, and a degree of greenness – even possibly some high spirits – may be accepted in a four-year-old novice; but they would be viewed less tolerantly in an Open class. Some judges are prepared to accept an 'on-going' buck in a novice; others are quite definite that this would disqualify any animal from being placed.

When the judge has seen each animal moving on both reins, the class is called into line in order of preference on their showing thus far. Each is then asked to give an individual show, and as this makes up a proportion of the sixty per cent for ride, training test and manners, it is obvious that the judge attaches great importance to it. Under the British Show Hack and Cob Association rules, the test should not exceed a minute and a half. Ideally, it will include a demonstration of walk, trot, canter, canter out, a simple change of leg in a figure of eight, halt and stand still, and a rein-back. Occasionally a competitor may try to impress with elaborate movements such as flying changes, but judges are advised to ignore these, except perhaps in a closely contested Championship. A simple show executed beautifully is infinitely preferable to a complicated one performed indifferently.

The judge not only takes the content of the show into account, but looks for the perfectly-schooled, supple horse that gives the impression of responding to the lightest of aids. The whole performance should be a delight to watch and persuade the judge that *this* is the horse he or she would like to ride in preference to all the others.

Common mistakes seen in the individual show include poor reining back, where the horse almost *falls* back with its mouth open and head up; striking off incorrectly; a horse that is obviously unresponsive and surly; one that is behind the bit or in any way unhappy in its mouth; exaggerated but ineffectual action, particularly at the trot. With regard to the latter, spectators (and some exhibitors too!) are sometimes surprised when an animal with a seemingly spectacular and extravagant action is not well placed. However, judges point out that the very extravagance of the pace in front sometimes distracts attention from what is happening with the hindlegs. These are often not moving freely, with the result that the horse is not really covering the ground as there is no impulsion coming from active hock action. A less spectacular but rhythmical pace in which both front *and* hindlegs are fully used is much preferred by knowledgeable judges.

The individual show is followed by the judge's ride. As in any ridden class, this is often the decisive phase. A point sometimes overlooked (although it should only affect the competitor indirectly) is the advisability of providing a steward who is competent in giving the judge a leg up. This is particularly important with a lady judge who may be very small. It would be a good thing if competitors themselves made sure they could perform this simple task adequately, in case of necessity. Consciously or unconsciously, a judge is likely to be influenced a little by any difficulty in this early stage of the ride. Judges insist that horses *must* stand for them to mount and there are those who, understandably, decline to ride an animal that will not do so.

Ill-fitting tack may also have a considerable bearing on the judge's final decision in ridden classes. Indeed, some judges have justifiably refused to ride a horse with a saddle that touches the animal's withers even before the rider has mounted.

Exhibitors should be conscious of the fact that, in many instances, the judge is riding their particular horse for the first time, and will probably approach it quietly, using quiet but firm aids. This is especially so in a hack class where the horses are often Thoroughbred or nearly so, and may reasonably be expected to be highly-strung. Although in the leading shows most animals are schooled to respond to light aids, in shows where the standard is less high a judge still does not expect to be confronted with a horse that needs to be kicked on, or is reluctant to leave the line. They like an animal that goes round the ring willingly, without cutting corners or pulling in towards other horses.

The ride consists, in most cases, of walking, trotting and cantering on both reins, and the judge will appreciate a horse that gives a comfortable, light, well-balanced, light-mouthed ride, with no stiffness or resistance. In an Open class, most judges ask for a rein-back, looking for a straight, willing, precise movement. In Novice classes, a rein-back is often omitted, as judges feel that free forward movement is more important at this stage. There is almost complete agreement that if a horse misbehaves during the ride, the judge should bring it back into line immediately — making it quite clear that schooling horses in the ring is not part of their duties.

Following the judge's ride, the horses are stripped and inspected individually, as in the hunter classes. When looking closely at hacks, the judge expects to see a head of great refinement, with fine skin and fine hair, through which the network of superficial blood-vessels are clearly visible. The bones must be finely sculpted, the eye big and generous, the muzzle fine, and the nostrils delicate but reasonably wide. The ideal hack head is fine and slightly smaller than that of the average hunter, so the neck should be a little longer and more elegant. Undue length, however, is considered a fault. The rest of the conformation is basically that of any good riding-horse, with, as has been mentioned, less substance and a little less bone than is required in a hunter.

Competitors are next asked to walk and trot their horses out as in a Ridden Hunter class, and one judge remarked that any suspicion of unsoundness will probably be confirmed or refuted at this stage, as the animals have been standing still in line for some time. A certain amount of distrust is engendered if a competitor takes a horse to the far side of the ring before trotting back or, as in the hunter class, fails to trot it in a straight line. The judge may suspect that the former is a ruse to give the horse extra distance to get going evenly and soundly before coming under scrutiny.

The vexed question of lumps, bumps and blemishes arises during the latter stages of judging, and although most agree that hack classes are primarily beauty contests, perhaps more than any other class except Children's Riding Ponies, they also agree that if a superb animal has a small scar or splint (provided the latter does not affect its action), it will probably still be put up above the slightly less superb animal that has no such flaw. If two horses are almost equal, however, the one with the scar or splint will take the lower place. With regard to fired horses, the judges are given clear guidance by the British Show Hack and Cob Association, with a rule stating: 'the showing of fired horses is actively discouraged, and judges are instructed to penalise them accordingly.' The British Show Hack and Cob Association also prohibits the showing of hobdayed horses.

Type, of course, is important in judging hacks. An attempt has been made to define the overall type that distinguishes hacks from, for instance, hunters. Within that type, however, there are variations, and personal preference plays a large part in the final decision. Some judges prefer the more Thoroughbred type of hack, provided it does not look too much like a racehorse; others, perhaps those with a strong hunting background, look for a little more substance; yet another group will choose the Anglo-Arab type as the perfect hack. In Small Hack classes, judges are very much aware of the danger of a pony type appearing – a type that not only shows evidence of pony blood (most commonly evident in the appearance of the head), but gives a rather pony-like, short-striding ride.

But in the end, as several judges remarked, 'judging is a matter of comparisons on the day'. The perfect hack is yet to be foaled, and if an animal that is a little too light, or a little too heavy, or in some other way just 'off-type' is put up, the judge invariably has a specific reason for it. It may have given the best ride, shown the most quality, or quite simply have had the best conformation in a not particularly distinguished class.

LADIES' HACKS

These delightful and elegant classes are judged in the same way as the Open classes, but with an even greater emphasis on faultless manners and an excellent mouth. The judge will, however, take into account certain features that tend to make a horse a better ride side-saddle. A very good front with plenty of length of rein is absolutely vital, otherwise the rider feels she is sitting right up on the horse's neck. Lean withers are necessary, and a slightly longer back is desirable as this allows more room for the larger saddle and undoubtedly produces a more comfortable ride in this class. A moderately dipped back, although regarded as a conformation fault, may also contribute to the rider's comfort. The judge has to weigh the merits of a good ride against any slight defect in conformation that in this special case, adds to the pleasure of the ride. In this she is guided by the fact that conformation is marked as part of the forty per cent of the marks, whereas the ride is part of the sixty per cent.

Judges stress the importance of the side-saddle being correctly stuffed. An unevenly stuffed saddle not only affects the rider's position and hence her ability to ride the horse with finesse, but can also make the animal's back sore very quickly. Insufficient stuffing at the rear gives the rider the feeling that she is about to 'go out the back door', while uneven stuffing often means a constant battle to stop slipping to the near side. Although these points are not included in the judge's marking as such, they inevitably exert some influence insofar as they affect the ride and to some extent, the horse's way of going.

While all hacks should have a fine, flowing action, this is even more important in a side-saddle class. Any suggestion of action that goes into the ground instead of over it is accentuated in a side-saddle, and a very vigorous trot that is over-full of impulsion and throws the rider about is, of course, deprecated. Suppleness is desirable in *all* riding horses, but an animal with a stiff back causes particular discomfort to the side-saddle rider and will be penalised accordingly.

As is well known, a horse that wins an astride class does not necessarily have the same success under side-saddle.

Some horses do not like the extra weight of the side-saddle or the different distribution of weight on their backs; others need both the rider's legs on them to produce their best performance and some, for a variety of reasons, adopt a curious crab-like way of going on the left rein. On the other hand, some horses go much better side-saddle. One reason advanced for this is that they will probably be ridden with lighter and more sensitive hands – a view that male judges and exhibitors in the other hack classes might dispute!

COBS

Cobs are also judged under the British Show Hack and Cob Association Rules at many shows, the classes being for heavyweight cobs not exceeding 15.1 hands, and capable of carrying 14 stone or more. Cobs are often described as heavyweight hunters on short legs, and they should be *judged* as hunters, but with special importance being attached to schooling, manners, and the animal's general suitability for the elderly rider.

As the class enters the ring, the judge looks for a sturdy, compact animal with a good head-carriage, that walks out well with plenty of activity and impulsion from strong hindlegs. Any tendency to break into a jog is penalised. When the class trots on, the judge likes to see an easy, swinging movement, with the toe well pointed. In times past, a moderate amount of knee action was accepted, and even expected, but present-day judges seek a much more hunter-like pace with the movement coming from the shoulder rather than the knee. Cobs are, after all, being judged as riding-horses with the emphasis on elderly riders, and a high-stepping action is far from comfortable, particularly at the trot. A smooth, rhythmical canter is also sought. Given the cob's stocky build, the gallop is not expected to show the speed of a hunter, but the judge wants to see a free, ground-covering pace, with no suggestion of galloping into the ground. The horse must pull up easily and quietly, and some judges test a cob's manners by making it stand for a short interval immediately after galloping. Several commented that unwillingness to pull up from the gallop is quite common even among the very best cobs.

In the individual inspection, the judge likes to see an animal with a noble head which is in proportion to the rest of the body; in addition to showing quality, it should give some indication of the generous, kindly and sensible character which is one of the cob's most endearing features. Bold, bright eyes and alert ears set well apart contribute to the typically intelligent appearance. The head should be well set into the neck, which, while sometimes a little heavy, should nonetheless be flexible and show a nice arch and some degree of elegance. Well-laid shoulders are absolutely vital, as would be expected in a riding-horse, with withers that are sufficiently prominent to keep the saddle in position.

The judge also looks for the cob to be very deep through the girth, short-coupled, with plenty of substance, and to show well-rounded, exceptionally generous quarters. A well-set, gaily carried tail is a cob feature.

Sound, sturdy limbs are obviously a necessity in a heavy-bodied horse that is expected to carry considerable weight, and strong, well-muscled forearms and second thighs are important. The knees must be wide and flat in front, and in the hindlegs much emphasis is placed on clean, well-shaped hocks that are placed well under the body. Short cannon-bones with plenty of good-quality flat bone leading to clean fetlocks that show no signs of puffiness are also demanded. The pasterns, although sloping, are not expected to be unduly long and the feet must be relatively large and open-heeled to carry the animal's considerable weight.

When the cob is walked and trotted up in-hand, the judge wants to see action that is as straight and true as in any good riding-horse, and the tendency to move with the toes turned out is very much disliked.

A cob judge looks for a comfortable ride at all paces, while not expecting the long, raking stride of the hunter. In spite of its height and weight, however, the cob should give a light, responsive, well-balanced, collected ride and show some keenness — without this developing into pulling. Above all, it should give a feeling of security.

Judges criticise some exhibitors for allowing their cobs to become over-fat. In an animal that is already sturdily built, excess fat is even more distorting than in the less stuffy hunter or hack; it also has the effect of making the horse roll when moving, thus giving an uncomfortable ride.

Temperament is of the utmost importance — a good cob ought to be virtually 'bomb-proof', although this does not mean that it must be sluggish. All in all, a winning cob should be a good-looking, good-moving, sensible, mannerly and safe horse.

Chapter 3

CHILDREN'S PONIES

RIDING-PONIES

Many British show ponies are crosses, or the progeny of crosses, between native ponies and small Thoroughbreds or Arabs. At best, they are exquisite animals, full of quality while retaining the intelligence and hardiness of the native breeds, and each year hundreds of them appear in Children's Riding-pony classes throughout the country.

A great number of Children's Ridden Show Pony classes are affiliated to the British Show Pony Society, and even those that are not are normally run on much the same lines, with the judges looking for the same features. There will almost certainly be wide variation in type and standard according to the size of the show, and an animal that does consistently well in local shows may never come out of the back line at a big county show.

The most junior classes are the two for Leading Rein ponies: the first for pony mares and geldings not exceeding 11.2 hands; the second for pony mares and geldings not exceeding 12 hands; both to be ridden by children of at least three years of age, but not more than seven. As the name suggests, the ponies are all led by a handler on foot. In both classes, it is the pony that is being judged, but as with all show classes, the overall impression does have some influence. One judge stated firmly that the appearance of the handler was almost invariably the first thing to catch the eye – if only because the handler is so much larger than the pony! If the handler is well and professionally turned-out, it so often follows that the pony is well worth looking at too.

Although it is the pony that is being judged, some judges are very conscious that in this class, especially at the smaller shows, it is not only the child who is having his or her first experience of the ring: if the handler is the parent, it could well be their first attempt at showing as well. Hence the standard of tack-fitting at all but the larger shows can be rather low. For instance, saddles are fitted so far forward that the pony appears to have a very long back, or the bit may be too big or too small. Although these points are not judged as such, they influence the appearance of the pony and the way it goes, and so may affect the final placings – albeit indirectly.

As far as the pony itself is concerned, the judge bears very much in mind the animal's suitability for a small beginner, so temperament and manners must be good. Most judges like to see a happy pony with a happy rider on top; that in itself tells them a great deal about the pony's temperament. Ideally, a quality pony is expected, with a small head, graceful neck and all the points of conformation to be found in any good riding animal. A fairly typical example might be a Welsh Section A type, perhaps with a bit of extra quality. Generalisations are dangerous (none more than those made about horses and ponies) but the pure-bred native pony, with the exception of the Welsh Section A, is not usually *quite* the type of animal the judges favour in these classes. There is, however, enormous variation and the types found in a small local show are almost certain to be quite different to those taking the awards at the major county shows.

In a Leading Rein pony (and in most children's ponies) a reasonably high head-carriage and a good front are essential 'confidence-givers', so that the child does not feel it has nothing in front of it. Too wide a pony (whether it be naturally so or because it is too fat) is clearly unsuitable for the short-legged little riders to stretch around. On the other hand, too narrow a pony may be unacceptably weedy – so a happy medium is sought.

The pony's paces should be smooth, and the stride neither too short and choppy nor too long – both of these being difficult for young children to sit.

In the individual show requirements vary quite considerably from event to event and from judge to judge. The minimum expected is that the pony should be walked away and trotted back, so the judge can see its action. Most judges do not want to see the handler doing *all* the work – they expect some indication that the pony will start and stop for the child, and the rider might also be expected to help turn the pony before it trots back. Some ask the child to dismount and lead the pony back into line, to see if it stands quietly and leads willingly. Just what is required will be made clear by the judge at the time.

There is some diversity of opinion about whether the riders in Leading Rein classes should be able to rise to the trot, but wide agreement that a child requiring a neck-strap or a strap on the saddle for support is really not ready to be in the show-ring.

The next class up from Leading Rein is for First Ridden Ponies, which must not exceed 12 hands, and must be suitable for and ridden by a child of nine years of age or younger. In this class, leading reins are not permitted and the ponies are to be ridden in snaffle-bridles.

Views differ a little about the type of pony best suited to this class. One opinion is that a first ridden pony should be a confidential 'nanny' type, although the rider is expected to be a little more advanced than the almost passive passenger of the Leading Rein class. Nevertheless, the pony should show some quality, and certainly must not be stuffy or sluggish – it must be a pleasure for the child to ride. A rather different judgement is that a pony in this class ought to be a gay little animal that is a thrill for a competent rider, and will give him or her sufficient experience to graduate easily to the 12.2 classes. All are agreed, however, on the absolute necessity for good manners and a good temperament, and in deploring the type of pony that needs constant kicking on. The 'patent safety', rather stolid plodder is likely to find itself some way down the line.

When the ponies are walking and trotting round the ring (cantering as a class is not permitted under British Show Pony rules), some judges expect to see a reasonably good outline and a little evidence of them being on the bit, or nearly so. Poking noses and trailing hocks spoil even the best pony, but *real* collection is not expected by any judges in this class, and a number are of the opinion that the young riders are not capable of doing very much more than sitting on top and urging the pony to go forward. Thus a pony with naturally good carriage will have a distinct advantage. There is bound to be a wide range of ability in a class of this type, with some very competent riders, and others with much less experience, and to what extent this influences the placings does vary considerably from judge to judge.

An interesting point raised is the practice of ponies appearing in both the Leading Rein and the First Ridden

Pony classes – with different riders, of course; judges felt that this is sometimes to the detriment of the pony, with consequent adverse effects on its final placing. Having been round the ring a number of times in the Leading Rein, ponies may become bored by the time they are taken in to the First Ridden class. The rider in the latter may thus have to work hard to obtain a reasonable show from the pony and is possibly not capable of succeeding. This is one explanation offered by judges for placing a pony well in the Leading Rein and down the line in the First Ridden.

In the individual show in the First Ridden class, cantering is permitted and the judge probably expects the child to walk and trot the pony in a straight line and then canter round the ring. Anything more advanced, such as a figure of eight, is not usually required. The pony must go away from the line willingly and not nap back towards the other ponies. Views vary about how much importance should be attached to striking off on the correct leg at the canter and there is a charming story of a pony that was placed well in spite of leading on the wrong leg throughout. When a disappointed rival pointed this out, the judge smiled and said, 'Yes, but didn't it go *beautifully* on the wrong leg!' Seriously, though, most judges prefer the pony to be on the correct leg.

Not all judges require the ponies to be stripped to be walked and trotted out in this class. But whichever method is used, they expect to see a pony of excellent conformation in all respects, with a small, very attractive head, graceful neck and refined (but not spindly) limbs. A certain amount of elegance is sought. If it is walked and trotted in-hand, the pony must move straight and evenly, and it is most important that it should be amenable to handling by a child.

The next step from the First Ridden class is that for

ponies not exceeding 12.2 hands, to be ridden by children up to and including twelve years of age. Here the judge looks for a well-bred pony of real quality and appreciable substance, but without heaviness. Most agree that it is difficult to find both quality and substance in this size, although they often occur in ponies with Welsh Section A or B in their pedigrees. Some judges look specifically for a slightly larger edition of the more confidential First Ridden Pony.

With regard to conformation, the pony should have a really impressive front, a beautiful, refined head and sound limbs with adequate bone. Above all, it should have at least some of the elegance to be expected in the classes for larger show ponies. Its paces should be free, light and airy, and it 'should move with the grace of a ballet dancer'.

As these classes are primarily beauty contests, scars and blemishes are frowned upon, but splints, *provided they are small*, are often not viewed very seriously. The difficulties of breaking in a 12.2 (even with a lightweight adult rider) without splints forming, are acknowledged in most instances.

As far as presentation is concerned, the judges expect riders to have the ability to get their ponies going well, with no mouth problems or head shakings; they also expect *some* collection. A puller is very much disliked as it invariably encourages bad hands in the rider.

It is assumed, at least in all but the smallest shows, that the riders have the elements of ring-craft, and know how to present the pony to the judge. They should know not to bunch as they go round the ring, and should understand when to produce the pony's best paces so the judge obtains the best view. Judges appreciate that it is not possible for the average child of this age group to maintain a pony in an extended trot for any distance, and most are content if they see the pace just once from each pony. It should be spectacular, with real extension, a slight snap of the knee and curl of the fetlock in front, and active hock action behind.

A very bad impression is given by children who try to *force* the judge to look at their ponies, by deliberately riding in front of other competitors or by trotting almost under the judge's nose. There is a world of difference between a child who presents a pony professionally (in the best sense of that much-maligned word) and the child who is arrogant and ill-mannered in the ring.

In the individual show, movements should be restricted to those which both pony and child can do well, but real competence is expected from the top riders. Most shows consist of a walk away and trot back, a short canter, and possibly a figure of eight. Some judges do not like to see a rein-back included, believing that the only way ponies should be asked to go is forward. Throughout the demonstration, they look for a beautifully balanced pony with perfect manners, who is responsive and obedient and clearly giving the child a lovely ride.

Galloping is not permitted in the 12.2 class unless the judge is unable to reach a decision about the first three ponies. They may then be asked to gallop one at a time. If this is necessary, the judge wants to see a pony that covers the ground effortlessly with minimum knee action, and that is well under control with the rider just having to open the hand a little to allow it to go on. Ponies that gallop with their mouths wide open, ears right back, and tails swishing do not impress. Ideally, the pony should be galloped down the long side of the ring, come back to a canter before the corner, then down to a trot and halt in front of the judge – maintaining smooth controlled paces and transitions throughout and halting with all four legs correctly positioned.

There are two classes for the larger ponies. The first is for those over 12.2 hands but not exceeding 13.2, to be ridden by a child of not more than fourteen years of age; the second for ponies exceeding 13.2 hands but not more than 14.2, to be ridden by a child of not more than sixteen. The judging of these two classes follows similar lines to the 12.2 class, except that the ponies may be asked to gallop during the preliminary judging (but not more than four at a time in the 13.2 class).

The judges are looking for the most beautiful, elegant, quality ponies in both these classes, with great presence and charm – even glamour – and excellent manners. Most like them to have some substance, but they should not look like small hunters. In the 14.2 class much less evidence of native blood is usually apparent, but in the 13.2 class pure-bred Welsh Section B ponies often do well. Perfect conformation is sought, with a small, neat, pony head, an elegant neck and fine limbs with adequate bone that looks as if it could stand some work. Great importance is attached to the presence of true pony type and although many entries have a significant proportion of Thoroughbred blood, judges are not usually looking for miniature Thoroughbreds that would be more at home in a Small Hack class, although this is a rather controversial point. Nevertheless, these 13.2 and 14.2 ponies are to the pony world what hacks are to the horse world and they are expected to show the same qualities of conformation, action and ride, while maintaining their pony character.

In the individual show a very high standard indeed is expected, with pony and rider presenting a well-balanced, flowing, attractive picture. Transitions up and down should be smooth and the customary figure of eight well and neatly executed. The most common criticisms made are of ponies being too stiff and over-bent, and lacking in free forward movement.

Manners in Children's Riding-pony classes have been the subject of many heated arguments and the British Show Pony Society specifically states that judges *must* take them into account in the placings. Most judges tolerate the occasional buck, provided the rider is in control, but persistent bucking is regarded as a breach of manners, as is napping. Any attempt at rearing will almost certainly result in the pony being asked to leave the class. It can be, and is argued that some badly behaved ponies are still well placed and this, regrettably, is true – but as in every other class, some judges are less strict than others. In their defence, they may have been concentrating on one side of the ring and missed the serious offence seen by every ringside spectator.

The British Show Pony Society also has a full range of Novice Ridden Pony classes. Entries for these must be four years old or over (three-year-olds may be entered after 1st July) and must not have won a first prize of £5 or over in an affiliated show (certain classes are exempted).

In Novice classes, the majority of judges are looking for genuine novice ponies of about four years old – not older animals that have never won and are never likely to. The same points of conformation are sought as in the Open classes, but with regard to behaviour, judges may not be too severe on a pony that is perhaps paying more attention to the crowd or to other ponies than to what is being asked of him. Nevertheless, a novice should be tolerably well behaved. Clearly, a young pony is unlikely to be able to produce the fully developed paces of an older animal, and the judge is quite likely to ask the ponies' ages before coming to a final decision.

Children's Side-saddle classes are an attractive feature of many of the larger shows. Judging follows the same pattern as for adult Side-saddle classes, except, of course, that the judge does not ride. A pony with an exceptional front and good head-carriage is essential, and it must be very well-balanced and possess absolutely perfect manners. A little bit of extra length in the back is an advantage. It is vital that the pony has been schooled to carry the side-saddle properly and that the rider can sit straight and apply the aids correctly.

Pony Pairs are always popular classes at many shows up and down the country. To win one of these hotly contested classes the ponies must be the same size and colour, have the same length of stride and go well together. If possible they should have identical tack – including saddles, bridles and browbands. The riders, too, must be well-matched and preferably wearing matching jackets, caps, jodphurs or breeches and boots, ties, and button-holes (if worn), and carrying the same kind of whips.

In conclusion, a judge, speaking for a number of colleagues, asked that the very elaborate bows performed by many young riders at the end of their individual show should be discouraged. Many judges find them faintly embarrassing and would much prefer a polite inclination of the head, or in the case of a boy, a simple raising of the cap.

More generally, judges do want to remind everyone connected with showing children's ponies – parents, producers, and most important, the riders themselves – that showing ponies should be a pleasure. Judges do not enjoy seeing bored, listless ponies that have clearly been 'over-shown', any more than they like the grim-faced, over-determined little people on top of the ponies, to whom a low placing is a major disaster. Not all ponies and not all riders are like that, but there is room for improvement.

WORKING HUNTER PONIES

Many Working Hunter Pony classes are held under the auspices of the British Show Pony Society; entries must be mares or geldings four years old or over who have not won £50 under British Show Jumping Association Rules.

The class has two phases, as in an adult Working Hunter class, with the ponies being required to jump a course of natural-looking fences and then compete in the showing phase.

Under British Show Pony Society rules there may be four classes:

1. Nursery Stakes, for ponies not exceeding 13 hands to be ridden by children of not more than eleven years of age over fences not less than 2 ft or more than 2 ft 3 in. high;

2. Ponies not exceeding 13 hands, ridden by children of not more than fourteen years of age over fences of 2 ft 6 in. minimum and 3 ft maximum;

3. Ponies exceeding 13 hands but not exceeding 14 hands, with riders not more than sixteen years of age, the fences to be 2 ft 9 in. minimum and 3 ft 3 in. maximum;

4. Ponies exceeding 14 hands but not exceeding 15 hands, with riders not more than eighteen years of age – the fences to be 3 ft minimum and 3 ft 6 in. maximum.

There are also corresponding Novice classes for ponies not having won a first prize of more than £3.

There are possibly few show classes that generate more heat and argument than those for working ponies. This is perhaps because they are comparatively recent events, and initially judges were less clear in their minds about the type of pony required. There is still a certain amount of controversy, the chief bone of contention being whether judges should put up show-pony types that barely answer the description of either 'working' or 'hunter', in preference to animals with slightly less quality but more substance and arguably more potential to do a genuine day in the hunting field. The judges themselves are far from unanimous on this. Some maintain that 'an ounce of blood is worth an inch of bone,' and that the quality show pony can and does stand up to work as well as its slightly less well-bred rival. The latter, on the other hand, is said to have the advantage of being less highly-strung, with a more sensible temperament so that it is less likely to be upset in the show-ring.

Be that as it may, one judge said quite firmly, 'I believe the word "hunter" was put into the title for a reason,' and complained that many ponies, irrespective of type, are presented so grossly fat that they could not possibly hunt or have hunted for a considerable time. In the earlier shows, at least, it is felt that the ponies should be hard fit – although it would be difficult to maintain this throughout a busy show season.

The jumping phase is always judged first, and the British Show Pony Society has laid down marks governing this and the showing phase. There are 50 marks for jumping and 10 marks for style and manners while jumping. Knocking down a fence incurs 10 penalities; the first refusal costs 15 penalities, the second 20, and the third disqualification. A complete turn in front of the fence counts as a refusal. A fall of horse or rider incurs 20 penalties.

In the jumping phase, judges expect the ponies to jump the course fluently and smoothly, neither going right into the bottom of the fences, nor standing so far off as to risk total disaster if they did the same thing over a solid fence out hunting. The show-jumping habit of 'hooking back' for a fence is not considered correct for a working pony. As manners are taken into account, pulling, napping, or disobedience of any kind will be penalised.

The second phase is judged much as any show class but with definite marks allotted. Conformation and freedom of action carry a maximum of 30 marks and manners 10 marks. The judges must include all ponies that jumped a clear round and those with 10 faults; they *may* call back all ponies that were not actually eliminated in the jumping phase.

Competitors are not permitted to change saddlery between the first and second phases, and some judges recommend that real jumping-saddles are not necessary as they cover up so much of the shoulder and some of the neck and can make even a good pony look very ordinary.

RIDING-PONY BREEDING CLASSES

A number of classes are held for Children's Riding-pony Breeding Stock, both under the auspices of the National Pony Society and independently. The range of in-hand classes include those for stallions, brood mares, and foals and other young stock. The judges look, among the stallions and mares, for the sires and dams of quality show ponies, and among the young stock, for animals that are themselves likely to make top-class show ponies. These classes are generally regarded as the real beauty competitions of the show-pony world, and the judges expect to see the very best of the many lovely ponies being bred in the country.

In the stallion class, animals with a wide range of

backgrounds are likely to compete – from small Thoroughbreds to Thoroughbred/native-pony crosses, Arab/native-pony crosses and descendants of these. Whatever their actual breeding, the judges require animals of undoubted masculinity, with outstanding quality and presence, great refinement and excellent conformation, suited in every way to be the foundation stallions for the Riding-pony classes. Temperament is very important, as is adequate bone and superb movement showing full use of shoulders and hindlegs. The stallions must, of course, show real pony type, and any animal that has even a slightly 'horsy' appearance is unlikely to do well.

As with the stallions, so with the mares, but with special attention being paid to great femininity. In these classes judges like to see mares with foals, and if an otherwise good mare does not appear to be doing her foal particularly well, it may be taken into account. This is rather a controversial issue, as there could be a variety of reasons for a poor foal.

When judging the foals themselves, the judges look for great quality, an exquisite little pony head, good limbs with bone in proportion to the size of the animal, and straight movement.

In the other young-stock classes, and notably among the three-year-olds, judges are quite often faced with two types of pony – those that seem likely to develop into the *real* show pony, and those that have a little more substance and might well mature as the rather heavier working-pony type. Personal preference may influence the final decision, but as they are Riding-pony Breeding Stock classes, some judges feel that this implies they should look for the genuine show-pony type.

Although temperament is clearly important in any class for potential children's riding-ponies, no great importance is usually attached to manners in the young stock. As one judge pointed out, 'They are nearly all highly-strung babies,' and some allowance must be made for over-excitement and juvenile high spirits. As in the other classes, excellent conformation, quality, presence, and straight movement are essential.

Chapter 4

MOUNTAIN AND MOORLAND PONIES

SHETLANDS

Although they are small, Shetlands can have enormous presence and this is what most judges like to see as a class comes into the ring. Quality too, is required. A good head with a big, bold eye is another important feature because, as one judge commented, 'If they haven't got these, it takes some time for their other features to impress you when they first come in.' A nice, long, active stride at the walk, and an interested, lively but kindly outlook also catch the judge's eye.

When the class trots on, the judge likes to see a good length of stride, a moderately round action, with no suggestion of the low, daisy-cutting movement more fitted to a hack. Native-pony judges (in some breeds more so than in others) emphasise that they judge the animals not only as suitable for riding and driving, but as ponies that should have genuine native features which contribute to their survival in their natural habitat. Thus a low, daisy-cutting action would be useless and even dangerous in a native pony travelling over the rough, uneven ground of mountain or moorland. Some knee action is necessary, but the movement should, as in any horse or pony, come from the shoulder. The hindlegs should also be raised with strong movement of the hocks. Most judges consider it a great mistake to breed and show Shetlands that move very low and close to the ground. Shoulder and hock action is invariably lost and the pony will go too heavily on the forehand. A well-made pony should move naturally in a reasonably collected manner – but one that has been bred to move very close to the ground almost certainly will not do so.

In the individual inspection, the judge looks for a Shetland to have a small, neat head, but one that is in proportion to the rest of the body. For some time the breed has been plagued by ponies with rather large, heavy heads, and judges are doing all they can to discourage the proliferation of such animals by placing them right down the line. The typical head is very broad between the eyes and the eyes themselves should be bold, open, and very kindly – great importance is attached to the latter point, as Shetlands are primarily children's ponies. Some judges insist that the ears must be very small; others are less fussy about this, provided the ears do not impart a 'horsy' look to the pony. All look for a well-rounded cheek-bone and broad, open nostrils. The ideal profile is slightly dished (concave) and judges do not like to see any hint of a Roman nose, or a profile that is slightly Roman and leads down to a rather long and protruding top lip 'a bit like a tapir', as one judge described it. The muzzle should not, however, be excessively square, nor should it be pinched and very narrow.

A well set-on head and neck, with a curve, not an angle under the jaw is required, as is a high head-carriage. The latter is important in a child's riding-pony to give some confidence to the small rider, and an animal that goes along with its head near its knees does not find favour with a Shetland judge. Some Shetlands have rather short, thick necks, but this is not acceptable in a show animal; it should be moderately long and show some elegance. The very wide chest sometimes seen is considered a fault. A well-laid shoulder and clearly defined withers are needed as in any other riding-pony, and Shetlands with thick, heavy shoulders will be penalised.

The judge looks for a short, strong back, strong loins and adequate length between the hip-bone and the dock, with no suggestion of drooping quarters. The tail should be set high. The body must be deep through and well ribbed-up, but judges are highly critical of exhibitors who show grossly over-fat Shetlands. This restricts active movement, makes the true conformation difficult if not impossible to see, and adds to the width small riders have to stretch their legs around.

Some Shetlands have such short legs on heavy bodies as to appear almost grotesque, and this type of pony will not be well placed. A long forearm is essential and while it should be well muscled, the bulging, bulbous muscles which make the legs appear disproportionately short are not true to type. Good, wide, flat knees are required, with a short cannon-bone and well-defined tendons, giving the appearance of great strength. The bone itself should be adequate in circumference for the size of the pony, but any suggestion of coarse 'cart-horsy' bone is disliked. The judge likes to see well-sloped pasterns and nicely rounded feet of a size to fit the rest of the pony. Boxy feet can occur even in an otherwise very good pony. At the back, the hocks must be well let-down, and the judge will be well aware that sickle hocks are an all too common feature of Shetlands. Stifle trouble is probably no more prevalent in Shetlands than in any other native breed, but the judge certainly looks for any sign of weakness or puffiness in that area.

A profuse mane, forelock and tail are essential breed characteristics which protect the pony from the rigours of its native climate, and a deficiency of any of these is penalised as being off-type. Judges do not expect a great deal of hair down the backs of the legs in the middle of summer, but a pony that lacks this altogether is untypical. The hair itself should be straight, and the crinkly variety found in some animals is considered a fault.

Colour arouses a certain amount of controversy in the Shetland world, and while some judges have a personal preference for black as distinct from coloured ponies, they are adamant that they do not allow this to affect their choice. Piebalds and skewbalds present special problems, because, like wartime camouflage, the patchy markings tend to break up the true outline. Most judges agree that they have to look very carefully at these animals.

Shetland judges are faced with the difficulty of a relatively broad size range, as the ponies may be any height up to 40 inches at four years and 42 inches at maturity. Some breeders have specialised in the 'mini' ponies, and to judge these in the same class as the larger animals is not easy. In addition, some judges have a personal preference for animals standing at the maximum or near-maximum height, believing that the ponies were originally bred to do a job of work and that anything under about 38 inches is bound to be less suitable. But they acknowledge that the breed standards allow for smaller ponies and they try not to let their own feelings influence their placings. There is, nonetheless, a notion that really good mini-ponies are comparatively rare. They are rather prone to have heads too large for their bodies, and although their bone measurement is adequate, this often inclines to coarseness. These features are, of course, also found in the larger ponies, but are

64

more conspicuous in the small ones.

When the ponies give their individual show, the judge expects to see straight, even movement and is severe on any animal that 'screws' its feet as they are placed on the ground. Although this fault is probably seen more in Europe than in Britain, it *does* exist here and is actively discouraged. Dishing in show-standard Shetlands is not a great problem (except in over-fat ones) but going too close is. There is a feeling that some judges would rather have them going too close than too wide, but from the point of view of the rider's safety there is little doubt that the pony going too close is the greater hazard.

In Shetland stallion classes the judge looks for ponies with a good, strong neck and masculine appearance, with a faultless temperament, and a high degree of presence and quality. Age is perhaps of less significance in a Shetland stallion class than in some other breeds, and quite old ponies still do very well in show classes. A back slightly dipped with age is not considered a great barrier to success, provided the pony still moves well and has a good set of limbs.

Shetland judges like brood mares to look feminine, and very kindly. They must not be too fat, and should stand over a lot of ground, with a good length of line underneath, but not too long a back. Some Shetlands are inclined to be stuffy, and a mare of this type is not favoured. A number of judges are very much influenced by the type of foal a mare has bred, even to the extent of placing the one with the best foal at the top of the line.

The usual difficulties are encountered when judging foals. In general, a foal that stands square on its feet, has an attractive head and kind eye, is well put together, and has adequate bone, is likely to head the line.

Judging yearlings presents unique problems early in the season, as Shetlands are the only breed that do not lose their coats in the normal way. Instead, the coat peels off in patches. Although the patchy look can be avoided by keeping the youngster in and grooming it constantly, some judges disapprove of this in theory, but can offer no other solution in practice to owners who want to show a yearling early in the season. Among yearlings that live out, few would have coats in real show condition before about mid-July, while those that are kept in and rugged-up, will clearly have a big advantage. A number of judges feel very strongly that even show Shetlands should be kept under as natural conditions as possible, to the extent that if faced with two ponies that were equal in every other way, preference would be given to the one that had obviously lived out, provided it was clean and well presented.

In Ridden Shetland classes, the judge looks for the basic points of conformation, but pays very great attention to impeccable manners, which are perhaps even more essential in Shetlands than in any other breed. They are so often a child's introduction to ponies and riding, and any display of bad manners or vice will not be tolerated. The pony must be calm and quiet and willing to do, as far as possible, what its small rider asks of it. If the rider is old enough, judges like to see him or her get off and get on again, in order to be sure that the pony stands quietly and is accustomed to being handled by a child. Again, provided the rider is old enough, the pony should be asked to trot, but most judges feel that cantering is not required.

EXMOORS

Of all the native breeds, the Exmoor is arguably the one

which appears (to the outsider at least) to show the greatest uniformity of type. There are a number of reasons for this, including the strict inspection to which every pony has to submit before being eligible for registration; the further examination of stallions at two years of age; the relatively small numbers of pure-breds in existence; and the Breed Society's firm resistance of the temptation to allow the raising of the maximum height from 12.2 hands for mares and 12.3 for stallions and geldings to 13 hands to cater for the riding-pony market. On the other hand, some finer, smaller animals have been bred (mostly away from Exmoor), but these are not encouraged by judges, who look for ponies at or near the maximum height. In pursuit of uniformity, one judge made the interesting point that when looking at a class of Exmoors, it was important not to be overwhelmed by the exceptional pony, but to choose the super-average, as the former would probably *not* be typical of the breed as a whole. Encouragement of the exceptional would possibly jeopardise the maintenance of breed type.

Thus, when a class comes into the ring, the judge looks for animals that show the breed characteristics of a well-made, strong-bodied, sturdy-legged pony with the typical mealy colouring of the muzzle, around the eyes, and inside the flanks (on darker ponies these markings can be dun, but they *must* be pronounced); the hooded 'toad' eye; and either a bay, a brown, or, more rarely, a dun colour with no white hairs at all. *Very* dark-coloured ponies are not favoured.

As with the Shetlands, Exmoor judges look for survival features, such as the snow-chute – a fan of longer hairs at the top of the tail which gives extra protection to the ponies when they stand with their backs to the wind and snow; the heavy top eyelid and eyebrow which help protect the eye from snow and rain; the reasonably prominent eye to allow for as much rear vision as possible; the short, thick hair which gives protection to the inside of the ear; and – a point often overlooked – the correct whorling and lie of the coat, which does not allow heavy rain to penetrate to the skin below. Strangely enough, a profuse mane and tail are not breed features under normal conditions, but the mane can grow on both sides of the neck. Some hair down the back of the legs is normal, but excessive growth tends to go with a rather coarse bone. Exmoors are shown in their natural state, without plaiting.

In Exmoors, as with most other native breeds, the judges appear to place particular emphasis on ponies that are going to be useful (as distinct from ornamental) and they look for conformation and paces that will be the most efficient for the purpose for which the breed is designed. One judge remarked that a pony's paces in the initial judging will give a very accurate indication of what will be seen later in the detailed examination of conformation. (This does not, of course, only apply to Exmoors.) For instance, at the walk the ponies should 'track-up' well (the hindfeet overstepping the imprints of the forefeet) and if one does not, it will almost certainly be seen on closer inspection to have faulty conformation. When they are asked to trot on, they can only, as one judge put it 'trot, and trot faster'. There is really no such thing as natural extension in the Exmoor and they cannot, because of the natural angle and lie of the shoulder, produce either the low, daisy-cutting action of the Thoroughbred or the high knee action of the hackney. If they can, it is a clear indication of lack of type.

The detailed examination should, then, be a confirmation of what has been deduced from the ponies' paces in the early stages of judging. The basic points of conformation are much the same as in any other riding-pony, but the judges do look for some special features. For instance, the nostrils should be markedly broad and prominent, to allow sufficient air intake, so necessary in a wild pony that relies on speed as a main line of defence. A wide muzzle is preferred for the practical reason that this will allow its owner to eat, say, three blades of grass, whereas a pony with a narrower muzzle might only manage two blades in the same time. Teeth are important, and Exmoor pony teeth are more upright than some other breeds, allowing for greater efficiency of grazing on the rough pasture of the moor; any departure from this is regarded as a fault. As in other breeds, over or under-shot jaws are not tolerated.

The Exmoor head should be very wide between the eyes, with the ears short. Long ears suggest horse blood, so are not acceptable. From the front view, the head is moderately short, but longer than, for example, a Welsh Mountain pony. In profile it should be straight with no sign of dishing; this is considered a fault and indicative of a certain deficiency in breeding. It is often allied to lack of bone. A good width (at least four fingers) between the jawbones is desirable, to allow for easy passage of food down the oesophagus, and for an adequate windpipe.

A well-laid shoulder is expected, and although the average Exmoor has less prominent withers than is found in a child's riding-pony, they should be well defined. Because the humerus in Exmoors (and in some other native breeds) is relatively long, the elbow lies further under the body than in a Thoroughbred, for instance. The forearm must be long and very well-muscled, and the cannon-bone really short. The joints are relatively large, a feature of primitive breeds which confers great strength. The hindlegs in Exmoors are nearly always well formed, and any weakness is heavily

69

penalised. Hard, black, sound feet are the rule, and heredi-
tary unsoundness is almost unknown. The ponies have
strong, deep bodies, but are not expected to be as close-
coupled as some other native breeds. A goose rump is permissible, and the tail is set quite low.

Exmoor stallions should be very masculine, and even in
the show-ring give the impression that in the wild they
would be herding their mares, ready to protect and defend
them if necessary. They should have a moderate crest.
Some tend to go too wide behind, a point the judges check
carefully.

The mares are judged much as in any other native breed,
with the judges looking for femininity and sound conformation.

In common with others, Exmoor judges have reserva-
tions about judging foals, feeling that the more precocious
have an unfair advantage. There is, however, less readiness
to judge solely 'on the day', as long experience of a well-
standardised breed enables the judges to predict a little
more accurately how an individual foal is likely to develop.
One point of conformation to which some attention is paid
is an adequate length of neck, as this is sometimes lacking
in Exmoor foals.

Judging of other young stock follows the usual pattern,
but allowance is made for the fact that the yearlings have a
very scanty forelock.

In the ridden classes, the judges concentrate considerable
attention on manners, bearing in mind that Exmoors can
be a bit high-couraged for very young children. There is
general agreement that the standard of presentation of
ridden Exmoors has improved greatly over recent years,
and the former 'rough-diamond' type is seen less and less.
The judges look for a pony that uses its shoulder well and

one with good quarters that it can use effectively to produce a free, workmanlike trot that covers the ground. Any pony that 'pulls itself along by the front feet' will be placed well down the line. Different degrees of trotting will not be expected in the ridden classes, because the shoulder structure, as mentioned, does not allow true extension. Exmoors are not so easily balanced and collected as some other ponies, and an animal that is allowed to use its *own* natural balance is more likely to go well for its young rider.

DARTMOOR PONIES

Dartmoors are judged primarily as riding-ponies, and are often described as miniature middleweight hunters with pony features, including a certain ruggedness consistent with their moorland background.

Initially, the judge looks for ponies of quality and presence, with a free, long-striding walk. When the class trots on, a hunter-type action is sought, that is straight, not too low, but with the toe well pointed. The floating action of a child's show pony is not considered appropriate by most judges, but free shoulder and hock action is expected.

The judge also looks for the breed characteristics of a small, short, pony head, with good width between large, luminous eyes that have a soft expression. There should not be any exaggerated tapering to the muzzle. Dartmoors have small ears, preferably with a slight in-curve at the tips – large ears appear in some of the larger ponies and are considered a fault.

The head must be well set on to a medium-length neck which should be slightly crested in both sexes and at all ages, and with a full mane. A clean, concave line under the neck is sought, with any sign of convexity being most undesirable. Well-laid, clean-cut riding-shoulders are expected, and the withers, while typically not very pronounced, must nevertheless be clearly defined.

Strong limbs are essential. In front there should be sufficient space between the elbow joint and the body (tying-in is a serious defect) and the forearm should be strong and well-muscled. Although the knees themselves are usually well-shaped, some of the breed tend to be a bit back at the knee, and this is always viewed with disfavour. While Dartmoors are not a heavy-boned breed, some are definitely lacking in this respect – one judge commenting that even with her fairly small hand she could sometimes encircle a pony's cannon-bone below the knee. Others tend to be much too long in the cannon, and their knees are consequently too far away from the ground. A small amount of fine feather at the heels is accepted, but a proliferation of coarse hair is not. The feet should be round, strong, and of a dark colour.

A back of medium length, with fairly well-sprung ribs, very strong loins and long, well-developed quarters leading to a well-set tail are required. Short quarters and low-set tails used to be much more common than they are at present. The tail should be full with long, straight hair.

The hindleg is expected to show all the qualities of a good riding pony, with strong second thighs and well let-down hocks. Sickle- and cow-hocks do appear, and if there is a weakness in the breed, it is a tendency towards rather poor hindlegs.

Judges like to see ponies of good strong colour, with black, brown and bay predominating. There are a few greys and the occasional roan or chestnut. A little white marking on the head or hindleg is accepted, but *only* a little.

Size is considered very important by a number of Dartmoor judges. The breed standard is a maximum of 12.2 hands, but many breeders find it easier to produce real type in smaller animals. There is, however, a strong feeling among certain judges that the breeding of ponies under 11.2 hands is damaging to the breed as a whole. Thus although there are some truly lovely small ponies shown, there is a move to discourage them even to the extent of placing them below a larger but less good animal.

Dartmoor ponies show two quite distinct types. The type likely to find favour at shows in the Dartmoor area are described as thicker, heavier ponies with larger heads, shorter necks, coarser shoulders and lower-set tails than those that are preferred by judges 'up-country'. Although heavier, they do not necessarily have better bone. These ponies are more of the harness-pony stamp, and while being perhaps rather plainer than the more showy type, they are probably tougher and arguably nearer the pony originally bred on the moor.

The second is the more quality riding-pony type – but it is important that these retain their native hardiness and do not look like little Thoroughbreds or children's show ponies.

When judging foal classes, judges look for straight movement, a very tiny, pony-type head, and good bone. At this early age, they do not expect the neck to be formed properly.

With regard to yearlings, judges complain that many exhibitors show their youngsters much too fat. They should be well-covered and fit-looking, not gross and flabby so that their shoulders are overloaded and their movement severely restricted. There is, as always, some divergence of opinion about yearlings that are higher behind than in front. A

73

slight difference in height seems to be acceptable, but in the opinion of many judges, a youngster that is really 'in two pieces' should be left at home. One judge mentioned certain specific features that may be acceptable in a yearling but not in an older pony. (These apply to other breeds as well.) For instance, a yearling will not be nearly so well developed in the neck or quarters, and may not have much wither. These deficiencies, if seen in an older animal, would be considered serious faults. Some yearlings are a little weak behind, but provided the actual shape of the hock is correct, this will probably be forgiven.

When assessing brood mares, judges look for ponies that are really 'broody' looking, and are not inclined to favour three-year-olds that have just been covered and do not look matronly at all. Some judges like to see a mare with a foal at foot, but will not go to the length of penalising one that is without. Straight movement is essential, but spectacular action is not expected. Conformation must be very good.

When looking at stallions the judges expect the very best the breed can produce. A really fine head is regarded as vital, with tiny ears and a bold eye; both stallions and colts should have very full cheeks. Stallions must have plenty of bone, and action that is rather extravagant while still remaining within the limits of what is suitable for a native pony. They must be masculine-looking, with an alert expression and plenty of fire and presence.

Dartmoors, although a small breed, are up to more weight when ridden than their diminutive size suggests. Nevertheless, judges are not very keen on large riders in the show-ring, chiefly because they cover up too much of the pony. Clearly, in ridden classes, good conformation is just as important as in the breeding classes and the judges also like to see the ponies walk out well, and carry themselves at both ends. Manners are taken particularly into account.

In the individual show a pony that is obviously giving its rider a comfortable, obedient and responsive ride is favoured, with special emphasis on a smooth, even trot and a well-balanced, smooth canter. It is not usual for the judges to ride Dartmoors in the show-ring, but very occasionally this may occur.

NEW FOREST PONIES

The larger New Foresters are often regarded as ideal family ponies because, although they may be up to 14.2 hands in height and should have the bone and substance to carry an adult, they are not too wide to be ridden by children.

New Forest ponies are not the easiest breed to judge; this is in part due to the size range (the smaller ones may be only about 12 hands), but chiefly because it is only comparatively recently that the breed has shown real signs of settling to a distinctive type. There are still ponies that show clear evidence of the enormous numbers of out-crosses to other native breeds and to Arabs that took place, some as recently as forty years ago.

When a class of led Foresters comes into the ring, the judges look for a quality pony that walks well, with a long stride and plenty of activity. Opinion about the trot tends to vary a little, depending to some extent on whether the judge is familiar with the ponies in their native habitat, or whether they are being judged by someone looking solely for a good mountain and moorland riding-pony. Judges from the former group will not necessarily fault a pony with a degree of knee action – although anything even remotely suggesting the hackney is unacceptable – because

75

they are conscious of the ponies' need to pick their feet up when moving across the rough country in the New Forest.

Judges looking for a good riding-pony expect the action at the trot to be rather lower, but certainly not to the extent seen in a true show pony. At the back the hocks must be well-flexed, and again, some judges do not object if the ponies pick their feet up a little. However, the judge who does not regard the higher action as a definite defect would, if confronted with two almost equal ponies, probably choose the one with the least knee action, purely because it looks better in the show-ring.

A rather similar dilemma faces some judges when they are assessing the individual points of conformation. New Forest ponies are inclined to have heads that are larger and longer from poll to muzzle than some other native breeds – although they still retain their pony character. A number of judges regard this as a breed characteristic and in no way detrimental, but others prefer the smaller heads more often seen on the stud-bred (as distinct from Forest-bred) ponies. The latter group of judges are faced with the choice of putting up a pony with a typical head above one with a more attractive head, and opinion among them is divided. No judge, however, likes a pony with the rather large ears that are a legacy from some earlier out-crosses to horses; nor will Roman noses or coarse heads find favour.

Most New Forest ponies have comparatively short necks, which help to balance the larger heads, so it is particularly important that they should have a well-laid shoulder in order to give the necessary length of rein. A thick or loaded shoulder is penalised, and in some ponies the shoulder-blade is too upright and so is in front of the withers – a very bad fault, as the pony cannot use its shoulder correctly. In common with most native breeds, New Forest ponies

76

do not have very pronounced withers (although they tend to be more prominent than some), but they must be well defined.

A deep body is required together with a short back, strong loins, and well-muscled quarters. The tail should be set well up, although the really high tail-carriage seen in some other breeds is not a feature of the New Forest pony. Drooping quarters and very low-set tails used to be prevalent in the breed, and while a number still remain, there has been a great improvement especially among the show-standard animals.

The limbs must be good, of course, and as the larger ponies should be capable of carrying an adult, plenty of strong, flat bone is essential. Lack of bone has also been a weakness in some animals in the past. The hocks, too, have not always been of the best, so the judges are likely to be particularly strict in their appraisal of the hindleg.

There is, as has been indicated, a considerable size range in the breed, and the ponies are usually divided into those up to 13.1 hands, and those from 13.1 to 14.2. The larger ones are, understandably, expected to show more bone and substance, while the smaller ones often have much prettier heads and should give an overall picture of an attractive riding pony for a child.

In their final assessment, the judges look for a well-proportioned, quality pony of some substance, with presence and manners. A New Forest judge, experienced in talking to Pony Clubs, uses the following series of 'shorts' and 'longs' to be sought when looking for a well-proportioned pony, no matter what the breed:

> Long from withers to point of shoulder
> Short from shoulder to elbow

77

Long from elbow to knee
Short cannon-bone
Long from hip to buttock
Short from buttock to stifle
Long to hock

The classes for New Forest stallions, mares and young stock are judged in the same manner as for other native breeds, with the judges looking for the obvious points of good conformation, but keeping a wary eye open for faults which can be present such as lightness of bone, straight pasterns, insufficient length from hip-bone backwards, drooping quarters and the occasional stiff or cow hocks.

In the ridden classes, the judges look for a comfortable ride which, in the largest ponies at least, gives more of a 'horsy' feel because of the typically good length of stride. They expect the hocks to be well underneath the pony – more so than is possible in the led classes – and that the pony should really 'go away from the back end'. Considerable account is taken of schooling and manners, with some criticism that not enough exhibitors take the trouble to school their ponies properly (a complaint not wholly confined to the New Forest breed). Some judges complain of very poor rides, with ponies falling in on the corners, and apparently incapable of leading with the correct leg. The New Forest pony with a rather upright shoulder is very heavy in front and 'feels as if it is going straight down to Australia'. But in complete contrast, a good New Forest pony can be a superb ride: well balanced, steady and with good manners, and this is obviously the type for which the judges are looking.

78

CONNEMARAS

Connemaras are usually regarded as hunter-type ponies, but having said that, judges rightly emphasise that they look for the genuine pony type, and not the rather polished 'little horse' that can creep into some of the larger native breeds.

When a class comes into the ring, the judge looks for a well-mannered, well-made pony that gives the impression of being tough enough and sensible enough to survive the harsh environment of its native heath. Individual features that are quickly noted include a pony head, a long, flowing stride, and a pony that carries itself well at both ends. Some judges look next for a pleasing *overall* appearance – an animal with a beautiful head and weak hindquarters is not what is wanted. When the class trots on, the judge expects to see a long, free, hunter-like action which comes from the shoulder in front, and although moderately low to the ground, shows a certain roundness. The snap of the knee and curl of the fetlock seen in show ponies is not typical of Connemaras, and a choppy, high knee action is considered a serious fault.

When it comes to the individual inspection, the judge looks for a head that is perhaps larger than some other native breeds of comparable size, but too much length is not liked and the muzzle should be quite short. There should be good breadth between big, kindly eyes that are not set very high. Some Connemaras have rather 'slitty' eyes, and this is not an attractive feature. The ears should be small and pony-like, but if they are carried well, a *little* extra length is not penalised.

There is some disagreement about the type of jaw expected in the breed. On the one hand, a rather strong, even 'jowly' jaw is accepted as typical, and developed as a result of the need to chew up rough, coarse herbage in the wild. Other judges disagree, and prefer a lighter jaw-line.

All agree, however, that the neck should be well formed, and not too cresty in the stallions. The breed normally shows a well-laid riding-shoulder, and this should lead to a well-muscled forearm of adequate length. The cannon-bone must be short, and as many of the ponies are ridden by adults, about 8 inches of bone is expected. The hindleg should be good, but sometimes is not; there is a tendency for it to be too short into the hock from the stifle, a fault, judges comment, which is seen more often in the English- rather than the Irish-bred ponies. Some ponies have second thighs, hocks and legs that are almost the same width all the way down, and in a number of foreign-bred ponies, spindly legs and small joints appear – all of these are considered conformation defects and are placed accordingly. The breed as a whole has good feet, neither too wide nor too boxy.

Connemaras have quite heavy bodies with considerable depth, and a rather long back. Although a nice level croup looks better, the ponies are inclined to have moderately droopy rumps which will not be penalised unless the droop is so pronounced that the animal, to quote one judge, 'looks as if it has been hit on the bum with a shovel'. As might be expected from the foregoing, the tail is set quite low and is not 'carried' at all.

As is customary, the judges use the individual walk and trot-up to see if the ponies move straight, and as a rule they do, with plaiting and dishing not being great faults in the breed. Most judges also watch the ponies as they turn to see they do not knock their hocks together.

Connemaras range in height from about 13 to 14.2

hands (14 hands is the upper limit recognised in Ireland) and there are two quite distinct types. The smaller ones are rather more compact, and some judges regard them as a more suitable riding-pony than the larger type. The latter is sometimes regarded as an all-purpose animal, and must be very active.

In stallion classes the judges look for great masculinity and for an animal that 'really breathes fire' but at the same time is well-mannered. Conformation must be good, and the action as near perfect as possible. As stallions, they should be better than all the others, according to most judges. One Connemara judge made an interesting observation about the stallion's action – and it could well apply to other breeds of horses and ponies. This judge looked with some suspicion at 'produced' action in an in-hand class, i.e. a rather artificial, spectacular action that can be taught to some animals but which may not be handed on to the progeny. He has found that if this action is also produced at a slower trot, then it is almost certainly a natural, not a produced feature. It should be said, however, that a more developed action would be expected in a ridden stallion, but this, too, should not be artificial.

Brood mares must be typical of the breed, deep-girthed and with plenty of room to carry their foals. Although they are not expected to carry themselves like a stallion, they should still have a nice, swinging stride.

Foals and other young stock are judged as in other breeds, but the judges had some interesting comments to make about yearlings – remarks which apply equally to youngsters of other breeds. Yearlings are clearly not going to be so balanced as the mature animals, but they should still be able to show the nice, smooth, long-striding walk. Their necks will almost certainly lack the curved top-line and look a bit 'empty' – which is *not* to say they should be hollow. Some are inclined to have 'a plunge neck-line' (necks that enter the chest a bit too low) and this is not a good point. At the stage of growth where they are markedly 'up behind', they will not move properly – although this differential growth is usually less obvious in the native ponies than in, for example, Anglo-Arabs. One judge gave a useful word of advice and warning: 'If the pony is lovely as a yearling, it will probably be ghastly as a two-year-old, and then gorgeous again at four. Conversely, if they are lovely at two, they're frightful at four!'

In the ridden classes, judges look for a pony with a good outline, and of course, expect more collection than in the led classes. Some riders try to trot their animals too fast, with the result that the neck goes 'inside-out', the nose is poked forward, and although the toes are often thrown forward in a manner that excites uninformed ringside applause, careful observation shows that this action is not correct. It usually results in the heel being down and the toe up, giving a frightful jar as the foot comes down to the ground. The canter should be elastic and smooth, with no suggestion of 'scuttering'.

When the judge rides, he or she expects a nice, smooth, willing ride at all paces. As the majority of Connemaras have good fronts, the judge should feel that there is plenty of pony in front of him, and as the breed is typically very well-balanced, this should also be apparent in the ride.

Any inclination to napping back towards the other ponies will be penalised, possibly more so because it is not a common trait in Connemaras. A judge suggested that this was almost certainly due to the fact that the breed as a whole is not unduly gregarious. Because of its origins in Ireland where the individual farmer probably only has *one*

82

pony, the herd instinct may be less developed than in, for example, the New Forest pony where herd life is important. The Irish Connemara mare is usually kept on her own in a field; when she has her foal, it comes with her when she is working, and although the foals are often turned out on the mountains to run in groups after weaning, their early formative life has largely been of a solitary nature.

HIGHLAND PONIES

As with New Forest ponies and Connemaras, judges of Highland ponies have to contend with a wide range of heights (from about 13 to 14.2 hands). The smaller ponies will obviously be a little lighter, but nevertheless judges emphasise that the breed is a 'strong' one and must have more bone and substance than most other ponies of similar size. They must also show great quality, and any signs of coarseness are very much disliked. Some judges admit to a temptation to overemphasise quality at the expense of substance, chiefly because they feel that beauty, or at least attractiveness is essential – and this is not always found in a very heavy animal.

When a led class comes into the ring, the judge looks for the true Highland type, irrespective of height, and for ponies with presence, brightness and plenty of activity. The short-coupled pony that walks out freely and fast, covering the ground easily and carrying its head, neck and tail well will immediately catch the judge's eye. When the class is asked to trot on, the foreleg should move from the shoulder and not from the knee, and at the back the hindleg must be brought well under the body with full engagement of the hock.

In the individual inspection, the judge expects to see an

animal with an attractive head, showing pony character, and with a slightly dished profile. A Roman nose is not acceptable. There should be plenty of width between the big, kindly, dark-coloured eyes, and the distance from eye to muzzle is short in the ideal pony. The muzzle itself is broad with wide nostrils. The smallish ears should be well set on. Highland ponies have a deep jowl, a clean throat, and the head must be well set on to the neck, the upper line of which should be slightly arched, but certainly not too cresty in females.

Highland-pony judges are among those who pay special attention to the traditional work for which the ponies are still used. They expect to see a good riding-shoulder giving sufficient length of rein, with well-defined withers being particularly important bearing in mind the steep terrain in the Scottish Highlands. Too many ponies give the appearance of lacking good withers, with a tendency to flatness, but these are frequently concealed by show-ring fat!

The judge looks for ponies with depth through the heart, a wide (but not excessively wide) chest denoting strength, and a well ribbed-up body. The back should be short, slightly concave, with strong loins and well-developed quarters, giving an overall appearance of compactness and great strength. The judge does not favour a herring-gutted animal, nor one with too long a back, the latter being considered a very serious weakness in a breed that is used extensively in hilly country. Low-set tails are sometimes seen and are a defect.

The limbs must be strong, with plenty of clean, flat bone (between 8 and 9 inches), and well-developed forearms and second thighs – especially important in animals that are used for carrying great weights. The forelegs should not be too wide apart. The judge likes to see broad, flat knees, clean-cut hocks and sound fetlocks spreading into good, broad hoof-heads. Some Highlands show signs of puffy hocks and these are, of course, penalised. The pony should be well 'let-into' its pasterns to give a sweet, springy action, but over-long pasterns are not liked in a Highland any more than in other breeds. The feet must be broad, hard, and round, with blue/black horn. The broad foot is essential for the soft ground on which the ponies often work, as it spreads the weight better. Boxy feet in a pony used for deer stalking are very much disliked, as they sink into soft ground rather rapidly.

Two of the most characteristic features of Highlands are their profuse manes and tails. The hair should not be coarse, and when the mane is washed, it should feel quite fine and silky. Similarly the hair on the legs should be silky, straight and not too profuse, ending in a small, silky tuft at the heel.

Highland judges accept any of the typical colours of the breed: grey, the various shades of dun and the occasional black or brown. There is some prejudice against chestnut, and no Highland pony should have any white markings.

In the individual show of paces, the judge will, in addition to noting the free action from the shoulder, check carefully to see that the pony moves straight, and that it does not show any of the breed's tendency to dish. Because the ponies are used so much for downhill work, and balancing heavy stags or riders, they are more suitable if they are not very close behind. The judge may therefore allow a little wideness behind at the walk, but at the trot will expect the hindlimbs to be contained within the pony – not swinging out from the hip, nor slack at the stifle or over the back. The trot, although free, is not expected to be the extravagant, floating action seen in some of the lighter breeds.

Requirements for the individual classes are similar to those in most other breeds of riding-ponies. The stallions must be masculine in appearance, with a good outlook and a kind, bold eye. They should be short-coupled, with plenty of substance, good strong quarters and near-perfect action.

The mares must be feminine-looking, showing real beauty and quality, and with depth through the heart. They should be roomy, and rather longer in the back than the males, without appearing markedly so.

In young-stock classes, the judge looks for animals that have not grown too precociously for their age, yet appear 'scopey' enough for satisfactory future development. An over-topped pony on inadequate limbs will certainly finish up right down the line. Good, straight action and good feet are just as important at this early age as later on. Judges comment that too many youngsters are shown with a great deal too much condition on them, making them appear heavy and stuffy, and with the beginnings of the loaded shoulders sometimes seen in the mature animals.

In spite of their build, Highland ponies make excellent rides. What they lack in speed they should more than compensate for in comfort, and on no account should they be heavy on the hand.

FELL PONIES

When a class of Fell ponies enters the ring, the judge looks for an animal that has great presence, quality and a bright outlook, and carries itself well with its head up. It must have Fell characteristics; one of the most immediately obvious of these is an active, ground-covering walk, of particular importance in the shepherding work they so often

This fine example of a heavyweight show hunter has the limbs to give a superb cross-country ride. The second thigh is especially well developed.

A hunter foal with plenty of scope and looking as if it should mature well.

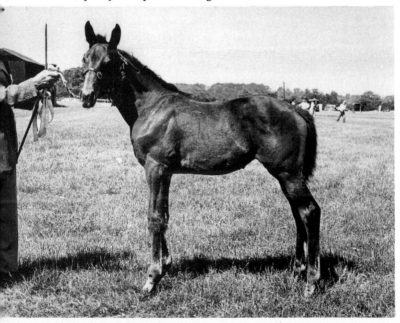

This good example of a Cleveland Bay mare has excellent legs and feet.

A charming hack showing the required elegance, quality and presence. It also has a very good length stride.

The slight Roman nose does not detract from the kindly expression of this cob. He is well up to weight and a good, strong colour.

A really lovely child's pony showing great quality, a superb shoulder and fine limbs.

This working hunter pony looks comfortable and happy, and it is good to see the young rider looking up and ahead, instead of down.

A most attractive Shetland with a lovely, slightly mischievous expression. The pony has a superb front and shows that the breed is well up to weight for its size.

The mealy nose and toad eye show clearly in this Exmoor pony. He has a good set of limbs and nice quarters.

A typical Dartmoor pony with a delightful head and tiny ears. A well-balanced pony with a good length of rein.

A good example of a New Forest pony. His head is more of the pony type than is found in some specimens of the breed.

A well-proportioned Connemara mare, standing over a lot of ground.

A well-proportioned Highland pony showing the long mane and forelock typical of the breed.

This good, riding type of Fell pony has a fine shoulder and plenty of bone.

A strongly built, short-coupled and very nice Dales mare. The feathering shows clearly.
A Welsh Mountain pony showing the beautiful eye and good front typical of the breed.

This Welsh Section B pony has the necessary good bone and is well let down.

A Welsh Cob (Section C).

A fine Arab stallion showing all the features of the breed, including the very fine muzzle and the low-set eye. He has a beautiful head and shoulder.

A fine Welsh Cob (Section D) with a very nice outlook and a particularly attractive head. The strength of the animal is obvious.

An Arab mare and her foal showing the charming gaiety of spirit and outlook so typical of the breed. The banner-like carriage of the tail shows well.

This two-year-old Anglo-Arab colt has a fine front, good limbs and the presence typical of the breed.

A splendid line-up of Shires; note their generous feathering.

A splendid Clydesdale showing the strength and compactness of the breed. Note the white markings on the underside of the body – a feature accepted in the Clydesdale but not in the Shire.

'Long, low, and wide' – an apt description of this pair of Suffolks.

The enormous strength of the Percheron shows very clearly in this fine animal. Note the clean legs without feathering.

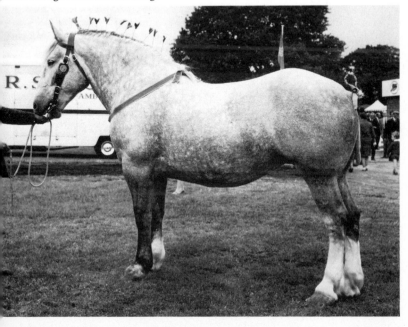

A good example of a Quarter Horse stallion showing the characteristic strong quarters and heavy muscling.

A Palomino going very kindly in harness.

A well-marked Appaloosa yearling colt.

A tandem going exceptionally well together.

A good hackney showing most of the qualities of the breed, including an excellent shoulder.

A Western rider showing that it is perfectly possible to look neat and well turned-out for this style of riding.

perform. When the ponies are asked to trot on, the judge wants to see a well-balanced, active pace, with the pony really striding away. Some knee action is expected, but it must not be an 'up-and-down' pace, nor should the whole of the shoe be visible when the foot is picked up. Behind, the judge wants to see well-flexed hocks, bringing the hindlegs right under the body. A low, daisy-cutting action is not typical and would be regarded as off-type.

The typical Fell pony for which the judge looks is a strong, hardy-looking animal with a small, pony head that has a well-chiselled outline. The forehead should be broad and taper to the nose which has large, distended nostrils. The eyes should be large, bold and prominent, with plenty of width between them. A heavy head or Roman nose will be penalised. The throat should be fine, showing no sign of coarseness, and the neck must be of a good length, showing strength without heaviness. This, combined with a well-laid riding-shoulder (which must on no account be loaded at the point) gives the good length of rein so important in any riding-pony, and even more so in one that is much used in steep terrain. In this regard, well-defined but not too fine withers are also essential, to stop the saddle slipping forward. The mane is typically long and profuse, and although not coarse, should not be really silky.

An over-wide chest is not desirable. The body should be deep through the heart, with well-rounded ribs from shoulder to flank, and the back not over-long. Fells are sometimes said to have an 'extra' rib which makes the shepherd's pony much more comfortable to ride, but it should still be short-coupled to give the necessary strength. The judge also looks for well-muscled, strong, squarish hindquarters, with a well set-on tail of profuse hair that is left to grow long.

When examining the limbs, the judge looks for a strong,

well-muscled forearm, big, flat knees, a flat cannon-bone measuring *at least* 8 inches (and it may be up to as much as 10 inches) with no hint of being tied in below the knee. The feet are, of course, vitally important, and must be of a good size, round, well-formed and open at the heel – their size facilitating passage over soft ground. The hoof must be of the characteristic blue horn; white feet are considered a fault. A moderately well-sloped pastern is wanted, and the judge will mark down any pony with the rather straight ones sometimes seen in Fells. In the hindleg the judge looks for muscular thighs and second thighs, with well let-down, clean-cut hocks, turning neither in nor out, and with good solid bone below. When making the individual inspection, it is invariably necessary for the judge to lift the thick tail to see that the hindlegs are placed correctly, as Fells are occasionally a bit wide behind. The legs should have fine feathering at the heel, but much of this may be cast during the summer, leaving only a tuft at the heel point. During the winter, however, it is important as protection against snow and rain on the hills.

The judge notes the colour of each pony carefully. Black, brown and bay are the most common, with a few greys, and although whole-coloured ponies are preferred, a small snip of white on the hindleg or a small white star is permitted. Chestnuts, piebalds and skewbalds are barred.

Fell ponies must not be over 14 hands in height, and may, in a few instances, be as small as 12.2. There are different types of Fells, ranging from the old-fashioned sort still used on hill farms that are smaller and sturdier, with short, thick necks and inclined to be stuffy, to the 'riding' type that is lighter altogether, often with less bone, and less hair in mane, tail and feathers. The judge prefers a pony that is somewhere in between these two extremes; the stuffy type is not really a show pony and the lighter type, although often a beautiful mover, is not regarded as a true Fell type, as it lacks the necessary substance that is so important to the breed.

In brood-mare classes, the judge looks for a mare that shows all the breed characteristics, as well as distinct femininity. As they are often shown straight off the Fells and not specially 'got up' for the show-ring, this must be taken into account by the judge.

Stallions too, must be of excellent conformation, not too heavy, and with a moderate crest. The judge should be able to imagine them as look-out post on the Fells, guarding their mares against possible danger. Any animal lacking in masculinity would certainly not conjure up that kind of picture. In the Fell breed, colts of two years and upwards are not permitted in mixed classes and must compete in stallion classes unless there are special facilities for the different age-groups.

Yearlings are considered very difficult to judge. Often a good yearling will not improve at all with age, while an awkward, gangling one possibly will, providing it moves well – and the judge is faced with the usual dilemma of how much to allow for future development. Judges do not like yearlings that are at all 'bull-y' about the shoulders, and are inclined to feel that a pony that is too furnished as a yearling will be too thick and coarse later on.

Two- and three-year-old Fell fillies are very mature for their age, and geldings take a year longer (approximately) to reach the same stage, making the judging of these classes far from easy. Some judges will make allowances for the difference in development and some will not – and exhibitors can only learn from their experience.

In Fell foal classes, the judge is more likely to favour the smaller, more compact animal over the precociously-grown one that may be over height at maturity. Foals of about two months should be well-rounded, alert little animals, moving well and with a good head-carriage. Many foals have lighter-coloured leg hair and feathering, but this will become dark or black when the foal coat is changed.

In former years, exhibitors in Ridden Fell classes were not expected to canter their ponies – chiefly because they were used extensively for harness work and in trotting races – and cantering was the last thing that was wanted. Now, however, the judge expects to see all three paces. If an individual show is called for, riders should demonstrate that their ponies can lead with the correct leg at the canter, and do a figure of eight with a simple change. When riding the ponies the judge wants a good, active, springy walk, a smooth trot, and in a well-schooled pony, a canter that is exceptionally smooth and comfortable. Choppy paces are not typical of the breed, and will be penalised.

In a Fell Pony Championship, the two- and three-year-old fillies are probably at less of a disadvantage than their contemporaries in other breeds, because of their typically early maturity. Sometimes a good young filly with its freshness and youth can beat a good brood mare that may have lost a little of its early bloom. In the inevitable range of ages and types in a Championship, Fell judges are careful to consider the stresses and strains on each age-group, especially with brood mares just off the Fells who are certain to be anxious about their foals. In addition, these led entries are competing against very fit ridden ponies and due allowance must be made for that. But in the end, the judges will choose the animal that is, in their opinion, the best Fell pony on that day.

The Fell Pony Society has devised a scale of points to

assist judges in making their decisions. These are as follows: height and colour – 5; head, nostrils, eyes, ears, throat and jaws, neck – 10; shoulders – 15; carcase – 20; feet, legs and joints and hindlegs – 25; action – 25; general characteristics – 100.

DALES PONIES

A Dales judge is immediately attracted by a strong, sturdy, compact pony that is alert and taking an intelligent interest in all that is going on around it. The judge also looks for a brisk walk, with free use of knees and hocks, and when the class trots on, a really active pace is wanted with quite high knee action and a 'flick' of the hocks. Dragging of the feet will be penalised heavily. Dales have always been famous trotters, and some of the older generation of judges tell of ponies trotting so fast that they went wide behind because their hindlegs were going past their forelegs! Even today, the judges like to see a really tough little pony that looks as if it could trot all day.

In the individual inspection, a real pony head is sought, with good width between bright, docile eyes, and small to medium ears that show a slight in-curve at the tips. The head should taper to a muzzle that is not *too* fine or narrow. Horsy heads seen in some Dales are probably a legacy from earlier out-crosses to Clydesdales, and are most undesirable.

The head must be set on to a neck that is not too short (short necks do occur in the breed, and are considered a fault) and leads to a well-sloped shoulder to give a good riding front. The withers are not very prominent, and the ponies are sometimes referred to as 'harness-topped', being rather flat immediately in front of the saddle. The mane and forelock should have plenty of straight hair that is neither very coarse nor silky.

Dales are typically very deep-girthed, with well-sprung ribs, a short back and strong loins leading to compact, muscular quarters. The tail, which should have a generous amount of straight hair, must be well set up.

The Dales judge will deal very severely with any pony showing defective limbs or feet. A very muscular forearm tapering to a wide knee is wanted, and the cannon must be short and show at least 9 inches of flat, flinty bone. Behind, broad, strong, clean hocks are required. A moderate amount of feather grows from about half way down the cannon-bone on fore- and hindlegs. Foot trouble is said to be almost unknown in Dales, and the judges expect to see broad, sound, hard feet of the typical blue horn.

Colour is important in the breed with black being the most popular, although there are some bays, some browns and a few greys. There are also a small number of dark browns dappled with black – known as 'hackberry'. White markings are not liked, other than perhaps a little on a hindfoot.

There is a certain amount of disquiet among some judges about the different types which have developed within the breed. The official height limit is 14.2 hands, but judges seem to prefer something a little smaller, feeling that some of the larger ponies have become rather coarse. A lighter, more riding-pony type with less substance has also emerged, and this does not appear to be very popular with the judges either, as they believe it is losing the true Dales substance and sturdiness.

Although Dales are used quite extensively as riding-ponies, there is a definite notion that cantering and galloping are not their best paces. Some can, in the ridden classes, be really uncomfortable; others, however, can produce a very pleasant ride.

Classes for stallions, mares, and young stock are as in the other native breeds – in all, a pleasant, kindly, sensible temperament is typical.

WELSH PONIES AND COBS

WELSH MOUNTAIN PONIES – SECTION A

First impressions in a class of these ponies is vital, for, as one judge said, 'They must shriek Welsh Mountain Pony by their gaiety and tremendous activity, their flowing mane and proudly-carried tail, and their fire, dash and presence.'

Having watched the whole class walk and trot round, some judges like each entry to trot past individually, considering that in this way they obtain a better comparison of their conformation, action and balance than in the individual show and inspection that follows. One of the outstanding characteristics of the Welsh Mountain pony is its great freedom of movement at all paces, and in the trot the judge looks for immense activity of the hock, which is brought right under the body and propels the pony forward. In front the leg must really reach forward right from the shoulder, with the foot first coming up before being fully extended. *Some* knee action is essential, but this should not be exaggerated or in any way suggestive of the hackney. Any dragging of the toe from underneath before extension (as is sometimes seen in show ponies) is just not correct Welsh-pony movement, and will be penalised.

In the individual inspection, the judge looks for a small head with a dished profile, a big, bold, luminous eye, and neat little pricked ears set well up on the head. The whole head must taper to a fine muzzle which has big, open, prominent nostrils. The head of the Welsh Mountain pony is often compared with the Arab, but some judges believe this is not strictly accurate, as the Welsh forehead tends to be flatter.

The jaws and throat should be clean and fine. Judges dislike ponies whose heads appear 'to be jammed onto the neck without any throat'; space for at least four fingers between jaw and neck is needed. There is some criticism of what appears to be a vogue for the type of pony that has a magnificent eye, but tends to coarseness through the jaw. The ears of these ponies are small, but lack a certain amount of quality and are often set on the head a little too much to the side. One judge observed that this type almost always has a 'cut-off backside', being unduly short from croup to tail.

The neck of the Welsh Mountain pony should be quite long, and although the mature stallions have a considerable crest, in mares it should be lean. In both sexes it must be carried well – an absolute essential in a child's pony so that there is something in front. Welsh-pony judges look particularly for a good front, so a well-sloped shoulder is indispensable and the withers, while being well-defined, should on no account be 'knifey' (narrow and very sharp).

No judge likes to see the pony's forelegs set too far under its body, and there must certainly be no suggestion of the elbow being tied-in. Plenty of well-muscled length from elbow to knee is necessary, followed by a flat, wide knee and short, flat cannon-bone. Strong, sloping pasterns of moderate length are typical, and well-shaped feet with no signs of boxiness are important. As in any riding animal, the judges look for a strong, muscular, short-coupled body with plenty of depth, and well-sprung ribs. A little extra length of back is allowable in mares, but stallions *must* be strong and compact. As has been mentioned, some Welsh

Mountain ponies are too short from croup to tail, and others have a rather droopy croup – but the judges look for hindquarters that are long and well-developed. A breed characteristic is the gaily carried tail, and any pony that is lacking in this respect will be faulted as being off-type.

The judges expect a good hindleg and hock, and it was remarked that ponies with a droopy croup always seemed to be sickle-hocked as well. In the walk up and trot back, the judges, as is customary, look for straight movers – and most Welsh Mountain ponies have little to criticise in this respect. Some are inclined to go a little close behind.

As in most breeds, there are different types of ponies. Welsh Mountain ponies' success as Leading Rein and First Ridden Ponies has, in some instances, resulted in the breeding of animals that some judges feel are really too fine when viewed as native ponies. There are also those that Welsh judges refer to as the 'English type'; as might perhaps be guessed, this is not intended as a compliment! These ponies are often very pretty, but differ from the true Welsh most noticeably in their movement. They are prone to going a little wide behind, and also to leaving their hindlegs behind them. Consequently, they do not have the typical 'reach forward' in front that is so characteristic of the best in the breed. They are inclined not to carry their tails correctly, and this, as has been remarked, is considered a definite weakness.

In a stallion class, the judge expects to see animals that are full of vigour and gaiety, with tremendous fire and spirit. Their conformation must be superb, and they should show a certain native ruggedness. They must not exceed the breed standard of 12 hands in height.

In brood mares, the judges want to see sweetness and femininity, and do not expect the fire and dash of the stallion. Nevertheless, the movement should still be ground covering, with the activity of the breed present in both walk and trot. Some mares with very large udders tend to go wide behind at a faster trot (this, of course, occurs in other breeds too), but it is usually obvious to the judge if this is their normal way of going, by watching them at other speeds and as they go round corners.

There is little to be said about judging Welsh Mountain pony young stock that has not already been mentioned with reference to other breeds. There was some comment from judges that in yearlings, the front legs were inclined to 'come out of the same hole', and that cow-hocks were by no means uncommon.

In the ridden classes, apart from preferring ponies that show real type, the judges are most particular about manners, bearing in mind that the riders are nearly all young children. All the paces are expected to be smooth, free, and flowing, and the ponies should not be overbent or in any way restricted in their movement.

WELSH PONIES — SECTION B

According to the breed standard, the Welsh Section B ponies should be a larger edition of the Welsh Mountain pony (but not exceeding 13.2 hands), with the emphasis on riding qualities. Many judges feel that not enough conform to this standard, and that in the effort to obtain size, type has been lost. Far too many lack substance and hardiness, and are becoming almost indistinguishable from the show-type riding-pony. There is a body of opinion that feels that the true Section B should be more like a miniature hunter in conformation than the miniature hack that is often seen.

Judges on the whole prefer a pony of around 13 hands,

with some substance and the real Welsh look. A good length of rein is expected – perhaps even a little more than in the Welsh Mountain pony – and they should have adequate bone in order to be up to carrying light adults as well as children. Faults likely to occur include overall weediness, a tendency to be back at the knees, and cow-hocks.

The action of the Section B ponies may perhaps be a little more of the riding-pony type than that of the Section A ponies – while now showing the extravagant 'toe-pushing' movement to such an extent. It must, nevertheless, be a strong, onward-going action without too much knee action, and the hindlegs brought well underneath at all paces.

Judges in Section B classes are often faced with the difficulty of choosing between a non-typical but very lovely pony, and a true Welsh type that has some glaring conformation fault that could hardly be overlooked. The decision is a personal one, and extremely difficult, with some judges being understandably reluctant to put up an indifferent animal even if it has type.

WELSH COBS – SECTIONS C AND D

Moving from the Welsh Sections A and B into the cob classes is like moving into a different world – and some judges (especially non-Welsh ones) feel they are almost taking their lives in their hands when they have to place one cob ahead of another. Nearly all horse and pony owners and exhibitors will defend their breed or type against all-comers, but the Welsh-cob owner seems more than any other to be totally convinced that not only are cobs the only breed to own, but that his animal is the best in that breed. Feelings run high, and it is a brave judge indeed that replaces an established winner with another animal that has shown better on the day.

The Welsh Pony (Cob type or Section C) is an animal not exceeding 13.2 hands, in which the judges look for as much substance as possible, with great strength, hardiness and extreme activity. All these must be combined with definite pony characteristics.

The Welsh Cob (Section D) is a larger edition of the Section C, and although it is sometimes described as 'a little big horse', it must not have lost all its pony characteristics, or have become coarse or common.

The judges are therefore looking for much stronger, sturdier animals than those in the Section A and B classes. However, they deplore over-fat exhibits that make it difficult to see what the true shape is and in particular, almost impossible to determine the existence or otherwise of withers. There may be some difference of emphasis between Welsh and English judges, with the English perhaps being stricter about a good length of neck and well-defined withers. The basic points of conformation are, however, much the same as in Sections A and B – but on a rather more substantial scale.

There are some differences. For instance, the head would not be expected to show the pronounced dish of the Section A, but any suggestion of a Roman nose would be heavily penalised. The expression should be kindly, and the head of the Section D cob, while being basically a pony one, should not be so small as to be out of proportion to the rest of the body. A hint of horsiness in mares may be forgiven by some judges, provided there is no suggestion of coarseness. In the Section C the head must show many more pony characteristics. In both there should be great width between the eyes, and the head should taper to the muzzle, but because of the larger size, this will not be so pronounced as in the Section A and B.

The feet, notably in the Section D cobs, sometimes leave a great deal to be desired, with poor horn, contracted heels and general flatness. Judges are of the opinion that this is not a breed weakness as such, but is almost always due to insufficient care at an early age. Bony enlargements and thickening of the fetlock joints also appear from time to time, but again, judges feel that this is probably more to do with over-feeding than any basic weakness.

Welsh-cob stallions, and most particularly the Section D stallions, should be as compact as possible, with tremendous fire and presence. The fieriness should never be allowed to conceal their very kindly temperament. A well-developed crest is characteristic of the cobs, but this should not be so coarse and massive that it falls to one side. Quality is essential in every detail of the stallion, with no suggestion of the cart-horse.

The action of both Section C and Section D cobs should be very active, free and forceful. The walk is not notably fast or long-striding, but is nevertheless a good pace with the hocks coming well under and the foreleg moving well from the shoulder. The trot, however, is *the* pace in cobs. It must be crisp and vigorous, with great activity behind and considerable extension in front. Some judges look for quite high knee action; others are adamant that although the knee must come up, any suggestion of it 'coming up to hit the chin' is incorrect, and that animals doing this will almost certainly not move straight. Some judges criticise the cobs, particularly the Section D, for various faults in their action such as dishing and plaiting. They believe that these are not necessarily inherent, but are caused, in some instances, by showing yearlings with heavy shoes that are left on too long. This, of course, militates against straight movement, and if continued can virtually ruin an animal's action permanently. Some Section C cobs are inclined to go wide behind.

In the ridden classes, judges prefer to see the exhibitors give a simple show, including walk, trot, canter, a simple change of lead, a halt and a rein-back. A careful watch will be kept on brakes and steering – they have been known to be less than reliable in some cob classes. In many ridden classes there are a number of stallions, more perhaps than in most other native-pony classes. One judge remarked that because the stallions are so aware of each other, and rather on their dignity, they do not always give of their best when they are being ridden round the ring all together. When each gives his individual show, however, there is often a dramatic improvement, and this will probably be taken into account, with the choice going to the animal giving the best overall performance.

Most judges comment favourably on the comfortable, well-balanced ride they have on both Section C and Section D cobs. Although they are heavy animals, they should not be heavy on the hand, and their natural balance ensures that most are not. Occasionally, judges do have problems with the Section D cobs being too round and fat for comfort, and with massive crests.

A brisk, gay, but not necessarily very fast walk is typical, and this should feel quite free-moving. In the Section C there should be a reasonable length of stride for the size. A good cob has a markedly active trot with great extension, and the judge should be concious of the hindlegs working like pistons underneath. A *bad* trot can be most uncomfortable and very choppy.

Cantering can sometimes be a problem, as there are still

those who believe that cobs should never be asked to use this pace, being historically supreme trotting animals. There are some delightful stories told of hunter judges (who are often asked to judge the ridden cobs at Welsh shows) almost purple in the face trying to get cobs to canter, while all the animals will do is to change into top trotting-gear and go faster and faster. The gallop, although not very fast, is a reasonable pace, provided the cob is the type that moves forward rather than galloping into the ground.

Most Section D cobs give the judges the feeling that they are riding-horses, while Section C's give the impression of being much bigger than they actually are.

MIXED MOUNTAIN AND MOORLAND CLASSES

Judging a Mixed Mountain and Moorland class is far from easy, and the judge must have a good knowledge of every breed, and a clear picture in his or her mind of the best type of each. The basic conformation is very much the same, but each breed has its own characteristics, and each, to some extent, emphasises certain features more than others. In assessing a mixed class, the judge does not so much pit each individual pony against all the others, as against the breed standard for each. Thus most will be asking themselves, 'Is that the *best* type of Shetland, or New Forest, or Fell – or is that Welsh Mountain pony a better example of its breed than that Exmoor is of *its* breed?'

Sometimes the mixed classes are divided into two or even three sections – with either Small and Large, or Small, Medium and Large Breeds – which makes it easier for the judge.

First impressions are of very great importance as it is

vital for the judge to be able to divide the ponies into their breeds quickly (not as easy in some instances as might be imagined). Most judges have one or two outstanding features for which they look in each breed, and the more typical the pony is of its particular breed, the more likely it is to catch the judges' eye quickly.

Chapter 5

ARABS

Most people in the horse world know that Arabs show certain anatomical differences from other breeds, which, to a large extent, give them their distinctive appearance. Not everyone, however, fully appreciates the degree to which these variations affect the conformation and movement of the breed. So before examining the individual classes, a discussion of the consequences of these unique features, and of the general points of conformation (both good and bad) taken into account when judging a mature Arab, may be of interest.

The head is proportionately much shorter than in other breeds, with the eyes set appreciably lower. The eyes themselves are big, bold, generous and kind, and noticeably protruberant. Small eyes are not an Arab feature. Plenty of width between the eyes is typical, and the profile must show the characteristic dish or 'jibbah'. This distinctive shield-shaped feature is formed by the frontal and parietal bones, and extends from between the eyes upwards to a point between the ears, and downwards across the top third of the nasal bone. It becomes less protruberant in the mature animal, but is nevertheless more prominent and more rounded in the mature male than in the mature female. The muzzle should taper, with not too much thickness through the nose, and the skin round the nostrils should be of fine, soft texture, with the blood-vessels delicately outlined. The nostrils themselves must be big, wide, and capable of the wonderful dilation so typical of the spirited Arab. The ears are small, although slightly longer in the female, and should be alert and interested. Some judges dislike an excess of white on the face, partly because it can have a distorting effect on the true Arab shape, but they acknowledge this is a personal prejudice and try not to let it influence them unduly.

The lower jaw structure has certain characteristic features: the outline of the jowl is larger and more circular and the V between the two sides of the jawbone is much wider than in other breeds — ideally with sufficient space to accommodate a clenched fist. An important aspect is the fine chiselling of the bones of the head and face, with any suggestion of 'fleshy' bone being a serious defect.

The setting of the head to the neck is one of the most distinctive Arab features. The neck should form a slight angle at the top of the crest, and from there join the head in a gentle curve. This unique angle is known as the 'mitbah'. The more pronounced the mitbah, the greater the ability of the head to move freely in any direction. The neck itself is moderately long — great length not being an Arab feature — and there should be a smooth curve, not a sharp angle, where the neck joins the head at the throat.

An undue dip in front of the withers is a fault, and while prominent withers are not typical, they should be sufficiently defined to stop a saddle slipping forward. The withers of ridden Arabs do, in fact, tend to be more pronounced, because the presence of saddle and rider help to chisel out the bones from the surrounding soft tissue. As the

Arab is primarily a riding-horse, a good, sloping shoulder is essential, although it must be said that this is sometimes lacking.

When viewed from the front there should be a V, not a straight-across muscle, at the base of the chest between the forelegs, and the chest should be wide, but not excessively so. The forelegs must be straight, with strong forearms; elbows that are tied-in too close to the body are considered a fault – room to slide the fingers between the elbow and the body is required.

The judge looks for well-developed, flat knees, and the small knees found in some Arabs, which make it difficult to distinguish the joint from the long bones, are a serious defect. The cannon-bone must be short, strong, and of adequate circumference. Arab bone is of greater density than that of other breeds, but this does not mean that there should be any *lack* of bone. While too much can make an Arab look coarse, a measurement of between 7 and 8 inches, depending on the size of the horse, is desirable. As in any other breed, clean, strong ligaments and tendons are essential. Sloping pasterns are required; a tendency to straightness being a defect in some poorer specimens. Round, open feet are important and the boxy feet seen all too frequently are severely penalised in show classes.

The back is short and level, giving the horse its essentially very short-coupled, compact appearance. This compactness is partly due to the fact that, unlike other breeds, Arabs have five instead of the customary six lumbar vertebrae (those to which no ribs are attached); also the vertebrae themselves are proportionately shorter; and most have only seventeen pairs of ribs instead of eighteen or nineteen in other horses. In addition, the Arab usually only has sixteen tail vertebrae instead of seventeen or eighteen, but this does not affect the length of the body.

The body must have plenty of depth, and because the ribs are rather more arched than in many other breeds, the barrel is more rounded. A long, level croup is typical, with the tail being set high and, like the mane, consisting of fine, flowing, silky hair. Strong, muscular and well-rounded hindquarters are sought, together with well-developed thighs and second thighs. The judges look for large, well-defined, well let-down hocks, that are neither exaggeratedly straight nor too bent. The average Arab could be said to have hocks that are slightly more bent than the Thoroughbred, but this is not necessarily a sign of weakness, it is just a common feature of the breed. As in the foreleg, a short cannon-bone and good feet are required. Arabs are frequently accused of having poor hindlegs, especially hocks that lack size, and the judges are likely to place horses with serious defects in the hindleg down the line.

That, then, is the basic conformation of the Arab, but having said that, there is always a vital additional requirement – the horse must *look* like an Arab. In other words, it must have the all-important attribute: type. It is quite possible for a horse to gain full marks for almost every individual point of conformation, yet somehow contrive *not* to look like an Arab at all! Like quality, type is not easy to define, and it is, to some degree, a matter of personal opinion. Most would agree, however, that to show good type, an Arab *must* have the characteristically shaped head, the short-coupled body, the flowing mane and tail, the air of refinement and quality, and above all, great presence. Size can have some influence on type. Very small Arabs may look like ponies instead of horses, while very large ones are inclined to become 'great, hairy, common animals', completely lacking the necessary re-finement.

Type must not, of course, be confused with different 'types', of which there are a number within the breed – although with the present-day practice of cross-breeding animals from many different countries, these are perhaps not quite so marked as in the past. Nevertheless, some distinct examples of the different types can still be seen in the show-ring, so a brief comment on some of their more obvious characteristics may be of interest.

The Egyptian or Desert type is inclined to be a bit more 'on the leg', a little narrower-chested, somewhat shallower in the girth, and sometimes lacking in length of rein. But this type almost invariably has an exceptionally refined and beautiful head, with great 'dryness' of bone, i.e. very fine, dense, exquisitely chiselled bone, which is an outstanding feature of the high-class Arabian. The Crabbet type, on the other hand, is described as being less leggy, and a more substantial animal altogether. The nostrils are usually exceptionally large and dilated and the ears somewhat longer than in some other types. Some judges describe Spanish Arabs as having inferior heads, and on the whole rather straighter shoulders, while the Polish type, which are sometimes a little plain as youngsters, mature with outstandingly good shoulders, limbs, croups and quarters. But, as has been said, these distinctions are becoming rather more blurred, and in any event, judges try (not always successfully, as they admit) to suppress their own preferences in making their final choice.

Turning now to the judging of the different classes, judges are obviously looking for as near perfect conformation and type as possible, but in certain classes place more emphasis on some points than on others.

Looking first at the pure-bred, in-hand classes – be they stallions, mares, or young stock – the judge's attention will be attracted to a beautifully turned-out animal which has great presence, panache and quality, and which quite simply stands out from its fellows and says, 'Look at me – I'm a beautiful pure-bred Arabian.' A good free walk with plenty of movement from the shoulder and with the hind-feet overstepping the marks of the front feet is essential. During the initial walk round the judge is, as with other breeds and types, obtaining the overall impression of which animal is likely to head the line-up, and at this stage too, a reasonably accurate opinion can be formed about those that are going to be placed at or near the bottom. The latter group nearly always includes those that do not walk well, those who do not fit in with the judge's personal opinion of what a good Arab should be, and those with the more obvious faults of conformation such as poor shoulders, lightness of bone, and poor hindlegs.

Having watched the class walk round several times, the judge will want to see each horse trotted out individually, and this, in the opinion of many, is the most exciting and spectacular phase of an in-hand Arab class. The trot should have that wonderful, cadenced, floating quality with the fractional moment of suspension that is instantly recognisable as 'pure Arabian'. It is important that the movement comes from the shoulder and the elbow, and that there is no high knee movement before extension. An impression of great onward-going freedom is required in the trot as in all paces. It is a characteristic of the Arabs that they hold their tails high like banners when moving at the faster paces, and the judge will fault animals that lack this feature. A few hold their tails to one side, and while this is not very attractive, it is not usually counted as a major defect. For this proudly flamboyant carriage it is essential that the tail is set properly, and this can never be so in a horse with a rounded, 'apple' rump.

It is important in both the walk and the trot that the handler should not hold the rein close up to the head, because although this can, when skilfully done, hide a 'nod', it also restricts the horse's movements and prevents him showing off his paces to the greatest advantage. Handlers should also beware, as in all in-hand classes, of trying to make their horse trot too fast. This, particularly in an Arab, is inclined to make them go wide behind.

When each entry has been seen at both paces, the class is lined up, usually in the approximate order the judge thinks they will take in the final placings. Most then inspect the class as a whole. One judge to whom I spoke always starts at the bottom of the line and walks up the front looking specifically for off-set cannon-bones; another does a 'troop inspection', walking along the front and the back, looking for straight legs, and at the hocks. Cow-hocks are not exactly a rarity in Arabs and there are judges who will, albeit reluctantly, accept this fault to some extent, *provided* the rest of the conformation is correct and the animal has the necessary presence and quality. Opinion is divided on this, and the exhibitor can only learn by experience when and when not to show an animal with this defect.

Having made the preliminary inspection, many Arab judges like to stand each animal out in front of the line for the individual examination. One judge remarked wryly, 'I like to stand them broadside on to the crowd; there are always many more judges among the spectators; they are always much more knowledgeable – and it's much easier to judge from outside the ring!' The animal is inspected from both sides; this is most important in an Arab class as the entries are shown unplaited, and the line of the neck is obviously easier to see from one side than from the other. The exhibitor can, of course, do a great deal to make the most of his or her horse at this stage. The animal should be encouraged to stand correctly, with one hindleg in advance of the other so that the judge is able to see both easily, and also to extend its neck (although not too much) to show its line and shape to the best advantage.

Following the detailed inspection, each entry will be asked to walk out and trot back, to remind the judge of the individual action, and to enable him or her to watch it from directly in front and directly behind to see if it moves straight. After this, the class may be circled again, before being brought in to the final line-up.

The routine for in-hand classes varies very little, but some discussion of the special features to be noted in the different categories is necessary.

Classes for young stock vary in composition according to the size of the show. The Arab Breed Show, for instance, has separate classes for senior and junior yearling colts; senior, intermediate and junior yearlings; junior and senior two-year-olds, and so on. Going to the other extreme, a smaller show may have one-, two- and three-year-olds all in the same class, making an extremely difficult task for the judge. However, nearly all judges agree that in these classes, as in others, the animals must be judged on the day. Thus in a mixed-age class of young stock, a judge does not try to compare a yearling and a three-year-old by attempting to predict what the yearling will be in two years' time – the winner will be the animal which, in the opinion of the judge, is the best in the class that day.

Having said that, some judges maintain that with year-lings it is desirable to consider their future development inasmuch as if the animals are too fat (as they often are) their bone growth, limbs, movement, head and tail carriage, even their breeding potential may be in jeopardy. Hence very fat yearlings may be placed down the line for that reason alone. As regards uneven growth, Arab judges are as divided as those in other breeds, but all are agreed that general conformation must be well up to the highest Arab standards. Various features characteristic of the year-ling stage are considered. For instance, a certain amount of juvenile slackness of the loins might not be regarded as a serious fault, unless it was pronounced or was clearly due to bad proportions. The judges expect to see at least the beginnings of a crest in yearling colts. Movement should be straight, although due allowance will almost certainly be made for the problems youngsters may have if the ground is uneven. The action will obviously be less developed and more 'on top of the ground' than in a more mature animal. Youthful high spirits are likely to be viewed with some tolerance in yearlings, even to the extent of allowing two or three attempts at trotting (if time permits).

Two- and three-year-olds are, in the opinion of some judges, much more difficult to judge than yearlings, as they are often going through an even more awkward growing stage. Two-year-olds in particular are often very disappointing, as they are prone to become rather coarse, or 'skinny and scraggy'. A well-produced two-year-old colt should show more crest than a yearling, but it should not be developed out of proportion. Three-year-olds often look more mature than they really are – a curious anomaly in a breed that in general reaches real maturity rather late.

Appropriate consideration is given if colts and fillies are

shown in the same class, and judges do not want to see a 'great, clumsy filly' or an 'airy-fairy colt'.

The Breed Show excepted, there are comparatively few classes for Arabian brood mares, and this, in the opinion of one judge at least, is a good thing, bearing in mind the high intelligence of the breed, and the ease with which a brood mare can be thoroughly upset and soured by too much showing. When judging the mares, most of the same points are considered as in brood mares of other breeds, but of course special emphasis is placed on the presence of good Arab type. Except for the Breed Show, most classes include mares of all ages and this does make judging more difficult. Judges often ask the age of a particular animal, and allowance must be made for the slightly dipped back and the distended abdomen resulting from continuous foal-carrying. Some judges make allowance too, for a slightly cramped shoulder in an older mare, but acknowledge that a younger mare not showing this feature is more likely to win.

In addition to femininity and as near perfect general conformation as possible, the judge of Arab brood mares will look especially to see that the croup is level, with no sign of the drooping outline seen all too often in the breed. This is never sightly or correct, but in a brood mare can lead to difficulties in foaling. It should always be borne in mind, at least from the judges' viewpoint, that the distended abdomen of the mare can make the back look longer in some animals and shorter in others – an optical illusion that needs careful consideration.

When it comes to movement, it must be as free and straight as possible, but due account is taken of the fact that it is bound to be slacker than in an animal in working condition. Nearly all judges make generous allowance for injuries and some blemishes in the brood-mare classes, as these do not affect the animal's breeding potential.

An interesting point made by one judge and echoed by others was the difficulty of concentrating on the mares when the foals were getting in the way. The wise exhibitor, therefore, will do all that is reasonably possible, without upsetting the mare or foal, to ensure that the judge has an uninterrupted view.

Arab foals present the usual problems, and although judges try to judge them on the day, inevitably they are to some extent looking to their future. For instance, most try and predict whether the youngster is going to have a good length of rein when older, and while it is easy enough to see the line of the shoulder, actually estimating how that is going to develop in relation to the neck is less simple. Equally, it should be possible to tell if any sort of wither is going to develop. In general, all the features of a good Arab should be evident in a foal. One judge explained: 'You just have to scale your mind down to the smaller animal.' Judges are inclined to be wary of a foal that is too precocious, feeling it may coarsen with age.

The most spectacular Arab classes are undoubtedly those for stallions. This is so in all breeds, but many people agree that there is a special quality about top-class Arab stallions that sets them apart from virtually all others. It goes almost without saying that they must be masculine in appearance and temperament, although the judges insist that this does *not* mean they should be roaring and squealing and striking out. They must be proud and fiery, with the absolutely compelling presence so typical of the breed, yet show the pleasing temperament for which the Arab is famed. In the not too distant past, some stallions in Britain appeared to have less than perfect temperaments, but fortunately these untypical animals have almost vanished from the showing scene. The stallion's conformation must be outstanding, with great emphasis on plenty of bone, and he should have a well-defined but not exaggerated crest. As mentioned previously, the jibbah will be more pronounced than in mares of comparable age, and the ears slightly shorter. When it comes to action, the mature stallion *must* show the elated, spectacular trot described as being 'deeper, more profound and more definite' than in mares and young stock, developed to its fullest extent. The stallion is also expected to have a longer, fuller stride at both walk and trot.

Judges bear in mind the Arab characteristic of late maturity. In a class of mixed ages (which is usual except at the Arab Breed Show) the four- and five-year-olds are certain to look less mature, and the judge will take this into account.

Arab Ridden classes are, by common consent, some of the most attractive in the show schedule. As the class enters the ring, the judges again look for an overall impression, with quality, presence and Arab type very much in mind. Manners are most important and a horse that is playing about, or having to be legged on unduly, starts at a distinct disadvantage. Judges are inclined to allow a little more freedom and freshness in a stallion than in a mare or gelding, but of course this must not be allowed to upset the other entries in a mixed class. As time is often limited, the class can usually be summed up quite quickly into the 'probables' and the 'unlikelies', so that the latter may be asked to retire before the judge's ride. However, it is Arab Horse Society policy for every entry to be ridden if possible.

As the animals go round the ring, the judge pays strict attention to the walk, as after all, this is the pace used to a considerable extent when hacking out. At the trot, the typical beautiful action is expected, but it should be a stronger pace than is normally possible in an in-hand class – partly because the ridden animals will, as a rule, be more muscled up, and partly because of the assistance they ought to be receiving from the rider. At the trot, head-carriage is important. Arabs normally have a high head-carriage, so considerable flexion is needed, but this should be as natural as possible and not give the appearance of having been 'bullied' into position. Length of stride is also important, as it must always be remembered that an Arab is a *horse*, and any suggestion of pony paces is most undesirable. At the canter, judges really do notice whether animals are on the correct leg; they say that when it comes to their own ride, they find that the animal which is reluctant to strike off correctly is stiff on that side. A change of rein is usual, and as in the led classes, it is necessary to see both sides of the horse because of their flowing manes. If the going is good and the ring sufficiently large, most classes are asked to gallop. A horse that really gets down to the gallop, as distinct from one that is 'on top of the ground', is favoured, as is one that can pull up kindly within a few strides.

During the judge's ride a variety of things are taken into account, but first and foremost, the animal must *feel* like an Arab, beyond any shadow of doubt. One judge described this as 'electric in their way of going, with tremendous gaiety and elation of spirit. Everything's an adventure (in the best sense) and they're never slopping along unless there is something wrong with them.' There should be a feeling of energy which, when used in the right way, is unique. Most judges will try the horse at the walk, trot and canter and possibly rein it back a few paces, looking, in the actual paces, for the freedom of movement that can be judged so much more accurately from the saddle than from the ground. Comfort is important; if the horse gives an uncomfortable ride, there is always some reason for it, which may have been missed due to the exhibitor's skill. Obedience, of course, is mandatory. 'The horse must,' as one judge smilingly put it, 'agree with what you are doing. But it must be made clear to an Arab *exactly* what you want, as he doesn't like to get in a muddle. That makes him panic – so aids must be simple and clear.' Naturally, the judge expects that the horse has been schooled to respond to these aids, but even at some of the larger shows, very green rides are still being presented. As a general rule, judges agree that while the ride is of great importance, they have probably seen enough prior to this to have a good idea of the likely placings. The ride itself is unlikely to effect any *dramatic* changes in their original opinion – they might bring an animal up from eighth to fifth, but are hardly likely to move one from sixth or fifth to first.

When the horses are stripped, certain points become more obvious than was possible with saddle and rider aboard. The most likely is a dippy back, which, other things being equal, has probably contributed to a very good ride – but is unacceptable in an Arab. The line of the shoulder is clearer, as is the length of the back. But in the final analysis, it is almost invariably the well-proportioned horse that comes out top in a ridden class, not only because it would give a naturally good ride, but because it will have been produced to give an even better one.

ANGLO-ARABS

The Arab Horse Society defines an Anglo-Arab as a 'cross from a Thoroughbred stallion and an Arab mare, or vice versa, and their subsequent re-crossing; that is to say, they have no blood other than Thoroughbred and Arab in their pedigrees.'

Judges assess Anglo-Arabs as riding-horses, and while expecting them to show some indication of their mixed ancestry, are not on the whole, impressed by animals that are either markedly Arab or markedly Thoroughbred. It is most important that they are 'all of a piece' – not all Arab in front, all Thoroughbred behind. Ideally, they should show the best features of both breeds, with the size and scope of the Thoroughbred and the beauty and strength of the Arab. There is some feeling that whereas a slight conformation defect in a pure-bred Arab might be excused if the animal has real type and outstanding presence, this tolerance cannot be extended to the Anglo-Arab, which must have near-perfect conformation. Judges also look for a kindly, sensible temperament and outlook.

Looking at the conformation in more detail, the head, while showing the great quality and fineness of the Arab, ought not, in the opinion of most, to be pure Arab in appearance. Nevertheless, an absolutely straight profile is not wanted. The horse should have a big, kind eye and the ears must be in keeping with the size of the head.

The Anglo-Arab must stand squarely on good limbs and good feet. More bone is expected than in a pure-bred, and the cannon should be short. Well-sloped pasterns of adequate length are required; the judges look carefully for those that are too long.

A good length of rein is essential, coming from a moderately long neck and an exceptionally well-laid shoulder. The withers are expected to be quite prominent. A few Anglo-Arabs are rather 'chunky' in front and this is most undesirable.

A good top-line is essential, with strength in the back and

hindquarters. There is a tendency for some to be too short-coupled; others are rather too short to the tail, i.e. the croup is too far back, and this is especially so if the horse is too long in the loin. The judge wants to see a well-carried tail; one that is clamped tight down probably indicates lack of freedom in the hindquarters.

The Anglo-Arab's action must be absolutely straight, and it may be every bit as extravagant as in the pure-bred. This can be seen in a number of the breed that have reached the top as show hacks. A 'chin-hitting', high knee action is totally unacceptable, and is sometimes seen in animals with poor fronts. The judges probably prefer a less spectacular straight-mover to one that is extravagant but not straight – and some can, almost literally, walk on a single track in front (a fault not confined to Anglo-Arabs).

Young stock are judged much as in other breeds. Sometimes, particularly if they have not been *taught* to move correctly round the ring, they go too wide behind. This is not usually regarded too seriously (and is preferred to those that knock their hocks together) unless the extra width starts right up at the pin-bones, and the limbs, although straight, are very wide apart and likely to remain so. Some dishing may also be forgiven in youngsters, provided it is not accentuated, as it very often means they have not learnt to use their shoulders correctly, and will probably improve with age.

In the Ridden Anglo-Arab classes, the judge expects a comfortable, enjoyable ride, with the qualities already described for hunters and pure-bred Arabs. The final decision often rests on whether the judge is more enthusiastic about Arabs than Thoroughbreds – or vice versa – depending on the type of ride the horse has given. Ideally, the ride should give them the best features of *both* breeds.

PART-BRED ARABS

Part-bred Arabs are those horses, other than Anglo-Arabs, whose pedigrees contain at least $12\frac{1}{2}$ per cent of Arab blood; the necessary percentage increased to 25 per cent for animals foaled after 1st January 1974.

In all but the very largest shows, classes for part-breds may include animals ranging, for example, from a 12.2-hand pony up to a 17-hand hunter type, and are thus very difficult to judge. At the Arab Breed Show there are separate classes for the 14.2 hands and under, which makes it less difficult and enables the animals to be judged either as pony-types or horses. However, in the more usual mixed classes, most judges look for what they consider is the best riding animal, irrespective of size. They hope that all entries are going to show some of the best Arab qualities, but with as little as $12\frac{1}{2}$ per cent Arab blood this is not necessarily so.

In addition to seeking the best possible conformation, the judges look for an animal with some quality, a big, kindly eye and a fine nose – all of which Arab enthusiasts hope have come from the Arab part of the pedigree!

Chapter 6

THE HEAVY HORSES

The Heavy Horse classes always draw large and admiring crowds – a majority of whom probably know little about the finer points of judging the animals, but who appreciate the size, strength and beauty of these 'gentle giants'. Because of the work performed by the heavy breeds, the judges look for a number of features that differ quite markedly from those required in a riding-horse. Indeed, some of the points of conformation desired in a 'heavy' would be positively detrimental to a riding animal.

Great rivalry exists between devotees of some of the breeds – particularly between the Shires and the Clydesdales – and the judge of a mixed class has an even more unenviable task than most. Heavy-horse judges seem to have a gift for apt, if somewhat forthright descriptions of faults in their own and other breeds, and so one or two have been included where appropriate.

SHIRES

Heavy-horse judges, perhaps even more than those of other breeds, look for those characteristics that ensure the animals are fit to do the work for which they have been bred.

When a class of Shires comes into the ring, the judge expects to see a horse that moves well, has clean, strong legs, an appearance of great strength and endurance, and which is also a typical example of the breed, showing no excess white markings or other features reminiscent of a Clydesdale.

Shire judges are likely to start their individual inspection at ground level and work upwards, being strong believers in the old saying 'no foot, no 'oss'. They want to see feet that are large, deep, solid and not too wide, but with an open heel, and thick walls. The coronet should be open and of generous circumference, and the pasterns relatively long and well sloped. A careful inspection will note any signs of ring-bone or side-bone – conditions not uncommon in the heavy breeds. The cannon should have plenty of good, flat bone (varying from 9–11 inches in mares, and 11–12 inches in stallions), and the presence of spongy bone is severely penalised. The cord-like tendons must stand clearly away from the bones. The judge looks for large, flat knees and for considerable length of bone from knee to elbow, with very heavy muscling. The hindlegs must have broad, deep, flat hocks, which when viewed from the rear should be quite close together. This is to facilitate good leverage when pulling heavy loads, and the judges will look carefully to see that 'you can't push a wheelbarrow between the hocks'. In former days, Shires were expected to carry a great deal of feathering on the legs, but today judges look for a cleaner leg. Fine feathering should still be present, with straight silky hair growing from the knee downwards in the foreleg, and from just below the hock on the hindleg. All four legs must be set well under the body.

Having inspected the legs and feet, the judge then examines the rest of the horse. A lean head that is in proportion to the rest of the body is expected, with large, prominent, docile eyes showing plenty of space between. The ears must be long, thin and sensitive. There is some diversity of opinion about the profile, and although the official breed standards require a slightly Roman nose, some judges are not very keen on this. Certainly a pronounced Roman nose would be taken as an indication of coarse breeding. The nostrils should be thin and wide.

The neck is expected to be reasonably long and slightly arched, but often looks shorter than it really is because of the heavy muscling. It is, however, proportionately shorter than that of the average riding-horse. The throat line must be lean and well defined.

Viewed from the front, the chest of a Shire must be wide, and there should be considerable breadth across the shoulders to give a good seating for the collar, with none of the streamlining so much desired in a riding-horse. Anyone who has read older books and articles on draught-horses will have noted that most authorities expected a much more upright shoulder than in a riding-horse. Modern judges, however, look for a somewhat more oblique shoulder (although still less sloping than in a riding-horse) with plenty of depth. A very upright shoulder does not provide a proper seating for the collar.

The chest is deep, with a girth of 6–8 feet in stallions of between 16.2 and 17.2 hands. The back must be short, very strong and exceptionally well-muscled, and on no account must there be any slackness or weakness in the loins. The judge looks for ribs that are round, very deep, and well sprung – flat sides being considered a fault which is both unattractive and suggestive of a weaker constitution. The judge also expects to see long, full hindquarters, massively muscled and well let-down towards the thighs. The tail must be well set; a goose-rumped animal is disliked and is not likely to be well placed. The strong rear-end is of great importance in a draught-horse.

Shires may be black, brown, bay or grey, but the judges seem to prefer the darker colours, especially black, and do not like white patches on the body (white legs are common). A hint of roan is permissible in mares, but this is not a popular feature, as both roan colouring and white body-markings suggest Clydesdale.

The action of the Shire should be forceful and with full and vigorous use of knees and hocks. The fetlock joint must be very flexible and the underside of the foot clearly visible at the walk. The horse must move straight, and at the back the hocks must be close together. Dishing in front does occur, and is penalised.

In a stallion class, the judge likes to see a fine, upstanding animal about 17–17.1 hands, of commanding and masculine appearance, and weighing between 1 ton and 22 hundredweight. Most feel that size is important in a stallion, and a few remark that in recent years, some exhibitors have come into the ring leading what they scornfully describe as 'pit ponies'.

In a Shire mare class, the judge does not expect such large animals. The average height is between 16 and 17 hands, with a girth of 5–7 feet, and typically standing on shorter legs than the males, with a bone measurement of 9–11 inches. The judge likes to see a feminine and matronly-looking mare, with plenty of scope, and a longer back; 'She's going to carry a foal, not a saddle,' one judge commented. The overall picture should be one of feminine quality, with free action.

Geldings too, may be slightly smaller than the stallions, but should not be less than 16.1 hands. The judge looks for a thick-set, well-balanced, active animal that moves well and gaily, and gives the impression of having the strength and stamina to do a good day's heavy work.

When assessing foals, some judges look at the dams very closely, to give them some idea of what the foal may be like in maturity. They also scrutinize the hocks with some care, because if these are too wide apart at this age, they will certainly get wider as the foal matures. They like to see plenty of length from the knee to the elbow, and a good, big foot.

Shire judges like yearlings to be attractive looking and very scopey. If they are too neat and tidy, they are unlikely to make a good size at maturity. An average yearling colt should stand about 16 hands or just over.

CLYDESDALES

Clydesdale judges maintain that in their breed they are looking for animals that are the most elegant and active of the heavy horses seen in British show-rings. The overall impression should be one of quality and weight which must not be allowed to become grossness and bulk. Indeed, the list of desired characteristics laid down by the Clydesdale Horse Society describes the animals as 'having a flamboyant style and flashy, spirited bearing, and a high-stepping action'. Being lighter and slightly smaller than the Percherons and Shires, Clydesdales are expected to show a livelier picture than their more substantial rivals.

When a class enters the ring, the judge looks for a very brisk, active walk, with the feet lifted high off the ground so that the sole can clearly be seen from behind. Breed type is important, and as the horses go round the ring, the judge looks for those standing about 16.2 hands, with white, flat faces, a longish neck, and forequarters that are noticeably higher than the hindquarters.

When the class is called into line, it is almost certain that the feet and legs will be examined first. Throughout the breed's history, special attention has been paid to perfecting these, and any deficiencies are severely penalised. The feet must be open, wide, and round, with wide heads and soft and springy to the touch at both corners. Hard hoof-heads are a definite fault, and any indication of constricted heels is most undesirable, as it could lead to ring-bone or side-bone. The hoof should be thick-walled, with a long, tri-angular frog, and with the wall about $1\frac{1}{2}$–2 inches beyond the point of the frog.

The pasterns should be long and slope at about 45 degrees from hoof-head to fetlock joint, and when gripped should be firm and clean with no superfluous flesh. These points, together with the correct shape of the feet and frog, were of the very greatest importance in acting as shock-absorbers in the days when Clydesdales worked long hours on the hard streets.

In the forelimb the judge expects a good length of flat bone below the very broad knees, with the latter being moderately close together. Viewed from the front, the forelegs with their strongly muscled forearm must be placed well under the shoulder, not protruding like a bulldog. From the side, they should be straight from shoulder to fetlock joint. Behind, the judge wants to see a good length from the big flat hocks to the fetlocks, with the shortish thighs coming well down. The hocks should be close together with the points turning slightly inwards – they tend to turn outwards with age in a working horse, due to the constant pulling action. Puffy or curby hocks are sometimes seen, and penalised, but perhaps not quite so much as they would be in a riding-horse. Viewed from behind, the thighs should show a good covering of flat muscle on the inside of the leg, but it should not be possible to see much daylight between. Round or broad thighs are a fault.

There should be a generous flow of straight, silky feathers from just below the knee in front and the point of the hock behind, probably more feathering than is currently fashionable in Shire horses. Coarse, wavy, or curly hair is undesirable.

Having satisfied themselves as to the state of the limbs and feet, and seen that the horse is standing close and square on its legs, the judge will turn his attention to the rest of the animal. The head should be of medium size, and in addition to the characteristic white down the face, should have a good, open forehead, good width between bright, intelligent eyes, a wide muzzle, and big nostrils. Wall eyes used to be more common than at present, and are disliked. The ears should be medium to long. A straight profile is typical, but if this is lacking, a slight Roman nose is preferred to a dished outline. The neck, with its flowing mane of straight hair, should be well arched, with a good crest in stallions, and proportionately longer than in Shires. A short-necked horse is disliked as it is hard to control in harness, especially in a team. Good, sloping shoulders, well muscled to provide adequate seating for the collar, are required. The judge looks for a short, very strong back, with well-sprung ribs 'coming from the spine like the hoops of a barrel'. Plenty of width across the loins is wanted, with no slackness, and the hindquarters must be wide, well-rounded, of good length and very muscular, but with not too marked a slope to a well-set tail.

The predominant colour among present-day Clydesdales is bay, with a number of strawberry roans; the black horses that used to be common are less so now. Four white legs are usual, and there is frequently a certain amount of white marking on the underside of the body.

When a Clydesdale is walked and trotted out the judge looks for a straight mover. The forefeet must not be thrown out at the trot, and although there should be some knee action, this must not be pronounced. Too much action behind is considered a fault.

There are a few special points for which judges look in Clydesdale foal classes. The youngsters' legs should be close together at each end – wide-set legs are undesirable – and when moving, the knees should remain close, but without touching, as should the hocks. The judges want to see a very well-set hindleg, with a perpendicular cannon-bone, and the thigh set at an angle of almost 45 degrees.

In a stallion class, fine, upstanding large animals are sought, with massive quarters. Mares should be a little less heavily built, with a slightly longer back.

One Clydesdale judge summed up the individual thus: 'If the horse is close and straight on his legs, the rest of his conformation will nearly always be right. If he throws his forelegs about, his shoulder is nearly always too steep; if he's not going close behind, he'll have too steep a rump, his hipbones will not be quite wide enough, with his stifles not leading into the thighs properly, and his hindlegs will not be underneath him.'

SUFFOLKS

Of the four breeds of heavy horses, the Suffolks are probably the most easily recognised by the non-expert. Firstly, they are *always* chestnut in colour, have no feathering on their legs, and are typically very heavy-bodied animals on short legs. 'Long, low, and wide,' is an apt description. The dictionary definition of the word 'punch' so often added to the name gives a good indication of the picture the judges seek: 'a variety of English horse, short-legged and barrel-bodied; a short, fat fellow'.

When the class is circling the ring, the judges like to see animals that are 'full of bounce and alertness', walking out smartly with a balanced, slightly swinging action. A good head-carriage is required and a pleasing outlook, giving the impression that the horse is enjoying itself. As in other heavy breeds, the feet should be picked up well to show the sole when seen from behind. Any horse with a coarse, hairy leg will be penalised immediately, as Suffolk breeders are proud of their animals' clean legs, with their consequent advantage of freedom from the skin problems sometimes associated with the heavy feathering of other breeds. A 'dash of hair' in the heels is not considered a fault.

When the class is lined up, the judge looks for a quality horse with a fairly large, intelligent-looking head, a broad forehead and full, bright eyes. A small amount of white or a star on the face is not penalised. The profile is typically straight, although a slight Roman nose would not disqualify, provided it was not pronounced. A few Suffolks have a very slightly dished profile, and this would not be penalised. There must be no coarseness of the jaw.

A graceful neck with plenty of depth in the collar is wanted, tapering to a good setting of the head. As in the other heavy breeds, a moderately sloped shoulder with strong muscling is required. From the front the chest must be very wide, with consequent wide setting of the front legs, but excessive width is not liked as it leads to a paddling action when the horse moves. The forelegs must be straight, and there must be no tying-in of the elbow — this is regarded as a very serious defect. The judges look for flat, wide, very strong knees, and particular attention will be paid to the presence of markedly short cannon-bones, which are a breed characteristic. Flat, good-quality bone is essential, measuring about $10\frac{1}{2}$ inches in the male. An excess of coarse bone is regarded as undesirable. The breed is sometimes criticised for being a little light of bone in comparison with Shires or Clydesdales for example, but Suffolk judges believe this is a fallacy. They maintain that the feathering of the other breeds gives the *appearance* of more bone, which is not necessarily present.

The pasterns must be fairly well sloped, and the feet round, strong, with a well-formed frog and no sign of a narrow, shallow or contracted heel. Some judges like to lie a rule across the shoe and expect the frog to be in contact with it. Horses with poor feet will be placed well down the line. The judges will certainly feel for ring-bone and side-bone, and although a hint of side-bone might be accepted, in general both these conditions will be penalised.

Suffolk judges look for a noticeably deep-bodied horse that is round-ribbed from shoulder to flank, and with a graceful line of back, loins, and hindquarters, the latter being of substantial width when viewed from behind. Some judges do not object to a little length of back, especially in a mare.

Good second thighs are wanted, and long, clean hocks — the latter are not always easy to find in the breed. From behind, the hocks should be close together.

A number of judges stand back and assess the angles of the shoulder, foot, and pastern, and are of the opinion that if all are at the same, correct angle, the horse will move well. If it has a short, upright shoulder, the pasterns will almost certainly show a similar deficiency. The action at the walk should be quick and springy, and at the trot the judges like to see a level, straight, well-balanced, gay movement, with *some* degree of knee action. However, 'no Suffolk judge delights in seeing a horse lift his knees up to his throat latch!' Some horses are inclined to have good action in front, but lack sufficient flexion of the hocks behind. Plaiting is considered a serious defect, but judges believe that the Suffolk's width in front is bound to cause a certain amount of dishing, although this must not be pronounced. Although there is bound to be some width between the forefeet, the hindfeet should be very close together, and a Suffolk should be able to walk up a 9-inch furrow quite comfortably. If a horse has too much width between his hocks, and is going between rows of sugar beet, he will, as was pointed out, 'kick out more than he'll hoe' – a practical aspect that will be taken into account.

There is some difference of opinion about the ideal size for a Suffolk. Some judges prefer an animal of 16–16.2 hands or just over, others look for something rather larger, but insist that the size should come from the depth of the body and not from the length of the leg.

Young stock are judged as in the other breeds of heavy horses, with the judges looking for well-grown animals that should make a good size at maturity.

PERCHERONS

There appear to be two schools of thought in Percheron judging at the present time, with one group favouring animals around or just over the minimum height of 16.3 hands for stallions and 16.1 for mares, and the others preferring horses a good hand taller. The former group maintain that the larger animals lack bone and general substance, and are inclined to have suspect joints and feet. Rightly or wrongly they attribute some of these troubles to the importation of certain French Percherons, and as many of these are bred with the meat trade in mind, insufficient attention is paid to feet and limbs. Even judges who prefer the larger animals admit that they can become coarse-looking, and that there is difficulty in finding ones that move really well.

Most judges look first for breed type, the most noticeable characteristics being the grey or black colour (dapples are sometimes preferred), the absence of feather on the legs and a prominent Arab-type eye. A high head-carriage is also typical of the breed, as is a very active walk which differs from the Suffolk in having a longer stride and rather more freedom of movement.

After the initial walk round, the judge makes the customary individual inspection. He looks for a head that has perhaps a very slight Roman nose, with no great length from eye to nose, but considerable width between the eyes. A deep cheek with a well-curved lower line is considered correct. The ears should be of medium length and erect, and the overall impression must be one of intelligence combined with docility.

The judge also looks for a strong neck of medium length, and a chest that is at least as wide, if not wider, than a Suffolk, and noticeably wider than a Shire. The shoulder should be reasonably sloping, but, as in other heavies, the slope is less than in a riding-horse although with considerably more muscling. The back must be short and very strong, and the body, although deep, is probably less so than the average Suffolk. The hind-quarters should show exceptional width, with good length from hips to tail and no sign of a goose-rump. Falling away behind is sometimes a fault with Percherons. Judges look for good breeching (i.e. thighs and second thighs) let well down to the hock.

As in all heavy breeds, the judge will pay marked attention to the limbs and feet. In front, the forearm should be well muscled, the knees big and flat, and the cannon short (about the same as in a Suffolk or very slightly longer). Good, strong, flat bone and sufficient of it is essential. The pasterns should be of medium slope and length; judges comment that some recent importations from France have been deficient in this respect, showing straight pasterns. The feet *must* be of good size, with the characteristic strong, blue horn. Great importance is attached to wide heels — a feature lacking in some of the taller horses.

At the back the hocks must be broad and clean, with adequate bone below — lack of bone behind is considered by some judges to be another fault of over-large Percherons. There is an inclination, within the breed, to have sickle-hocks and this is often seen in horses that fall away sharply behind.

The action at both walk and trot should be active and straight with a generous length of stride, contrasting with the shorter, snappier action of the Suffolk. Dishing sometimes occurs, but on the whole judges prefer this, which they feel is almost inevitable in a very wide-chested horse, to a pigeon-toed animal. The hocks should be well flexed and fairly close together.

Some judges will want to check that there is no sign of strong halt or of shivering. (The latter is a shivering of the limbs and cocking of the tail sometimes seen in heavy horses.) Others will ask for the horse to be backed up, so they can check that there is no trouble in the stifle.

When judging young stock, Percheron judges look for animals that are not over-developed at too early an age. They do not like fat foals, or yearlings that, while not having any great size, have matured too early. Slight plainness and commonness as a yearling is not necessarily regarded as a fault. Percheron judges, rather more than some of other breeds, are prone to look for potential, and believe the plain, slightly common youngster is very likely to develop well.

Chapter 7

QUARTER HORSES, PALOMINOS AND APPALOOSAS

QUARTER HORSES

The compact, short-coupled and heavily muscled Quarter Horses are a comparatively new addition to the British showing scene, but there are an increasing number of classes for them, as well as a Breed Show. Judging is conducted according to the rules of the American Quarter Horse Association, and in some respects these demand a higher standard of ring-craft and presentation than is seen in the average British in-hand class. Not, as judges are quick to point out, that these high standards have been attained by many British Quarter Horse exhibitors so far, but the British Quarter Horse Association is doing a great deal to encourage better presentation.

As a halter (in-hand) class enters the ring and proceeds round in a counter-clockwise direction, the judge looks for animals with an alert walk that covers a lot of ground. This is of special significance in a horse that was traditionally used as a means of transport in the wide open spaces of the American West, where riding all day was commonplace.

As in English classes, the judge seeks an overall impression of conformation and temperament, and in

Quarter Horse classes, almost irrespective of the horse's age, manners are judged extremely strictly. Any pulling back, neighing, rearing, striking out, or other forms of misbehaviour are severely penalised, even to the extent of the horse being (as the Americans so nicely describe it) excused from the class.

The individual inspection follows much the same pattern as in English classes, with the judge examining the horse from all angles, and then asking for a walk up and trot back.

The ideal Quarter Horse has a comparatively short, compact head, with a fine muzzle, and a shallow, firm mouth. As in other breeds, under- or over-shot jaws are not acceptable. The eyes are large and wide set, and must reflect the equable and highly intelligent character that is such a feature of the breed. The judge looks for medium-length ears, set wide apart, and always pricked, and a characteristic of Quarter Horses is the very strong jawline, which in some can become rather 'jowly'. The neck, which joins the head at an angle of approximately 45 degrees, is of moderate length and should not be markedly arched, or with too heavy a crest in a stallion. The throat should not show too much thickness, and plenty of width between the lower jaws is essential to prevent restriction of the windpipe in an animal that often has its head held low when working cattle.

Quarter Horses typically have long, sloping shoulders, and although they are very heavily muscled, this should be smooth and not bulbous. Medium withers are expected, which are well defined and extend back to allow correct and firm positioning of the saddle.

The judges look for a deep, very broad chest, and this broadness ensures the typical, wide set of the forelegs. The muscling on the inside of the forearm is long and very heavy, and should make a distinct and well-defined V-shape between the forelegs. The forearm angle is very open. The knees should be big and flat, and the cannon-bone very short, perpendicular, and broad when viewed from the side. Well-defined tendons that are clearly separated from the bone and from each other are essential. Quarter Horses give the impression of being shorter-legged than almost any other breed of comparable size. The pasterns should be of medium length and slope at any angle around 45 degrees, and the judge looks for an oblong hoof of a size proportional to the horse, sloping at the same angle as the pastern, and with a deep, wide heel.

A short back is an essential feature of the Quarter Horse, and there must be exceptional strength across the loins. The judge also looks for a deep-girthed animal with well-sprung ribs and an under line that is longer than the back, and does not rise abruptly to give a herring-gutted or greyhound appearance. The hindquarters, when viewed from the side or the back, must be markedly broad, deep and heavy, with particularly powerful muscling of the thigh and stifle, and down the hock. The hip muscling is expected to be long, and extends down into the stifle; the latter when viewed from the rear is the widest part of the horse. The judge pays special attention to the muscling of the hindquarters, as it is from here that the characteristic explosive acceleration of the Quarter Horse is generated. The croup should be long and slope gently to the tail. The croup and the withers should be approximately the same height.

Broad, flat, clean hocks that do not turn either in or out are required, and below these, the cannon-bone, pastern and hoof are much as in the foreleg, allowing, of course, for the slightly narrower shape of the hoof.

Quarter Horses may be any solid colour, but any spots, markings or colour that might indicate Appaloosa, Albino, or Pinot (piebald or skewbald) breeding is barred.

Quarter Horse foals are expected to have neat, compact heads, a reasonable length of neck leading smoothly into well-sloped shoulders, and to present a picture of the adult in miniature, although with a rather rounder rump.

In yearlings, the judges look for a good top line and strong, straight legs. The latter are most desirable, as generally speaking, if the legs are good at the yearling stage, they remain good throughout life.

In brood mares, the judges look, as in any other breed, for an animal that is feminine in appearance, and less heavy and muscular than the males, with a somewhat lighter forehand. A *slightly* longer back is accepted, and judges look for a good length underneath to allow space for carrying a foal. There must not, however, be any loss of strength in the loins.

Stallions are, as might be expected, heavier in build, and must look masculine and alert, and judges take specific note of manners and temperament. The breed is renowned for its docile, calm outlook, and a stallion (or indeed, any Quarter Horse) departing from this will incur severe penalties, and will probably not be judged at all.

In Quarter Horse Ridden classes, the judges require an animal that gives the appearance of being a pleasure to ride all day – which was, of course, the original purpose of the breed. A long-striding, free walk, a nice smooth trot that does not show extension (as this would not be a comfortable pace over a long distance) and a ground-covering canter, are the points most sought. Quarter Horses in ridden classes are not expected to show as much collection as would be required of an English hack for example, but they must be superbly balanced and not go on their forehands. Judges do not ride the entries in Quarter Horse classes – it is left to the exhibitor to demonstrate the horse's merits.

Although the basic conformation of Quarter Horses is the same, there are several types. What might be called the 'old-fashioned', cattle-cutting type is a small, chunky, massively muscled animal that looks broad from every angle. It has a very heavy jowl, a short, thick neck, an exceptionally short back, and huge, heavy quarters. Its legs were described by one judge as being almost 'muscle-bound' – the overall muscling is so heavy that really free movement is partially impaired because the forehand is so weighty. There are still some of these animals around, but the tendency in the United States show-rings (which is likely to be followed in Britain) is towards a rather lighter, Thoroughbred-type horse with more quality. In this type the head is finer, particularly around the muzzle, although the jowl is still moderately heavy. The neck, too, is finer, with a much better throat line. The shoulders, while retaining the exceptionally heavy muscling, are not nearly so loaded as in the chunkier type, and the back has lengthened slightly, but retains its great strength. It seems probable that judges of Quarter Horses in Britain will favour this type of animal more and more in the years to come. The type of Quarter Horse bred in America for the race-track, and containing a high proportion of Thoroughbred blood is unlikely to be encountered in British show-rings.

The original Quarter Horses were small – between 14.2 and 14.3 hands – partly because of poor food, and partly because their size made them handier for cattle work. The present-day breed ranges from about 14.2 to over 16 hands.

Ring-craft plays a very great part in Quarter Horse classes in the United States, and as there is a commendable move to encourage the same high standards in British Quarter Horse classes, a few comments about the methods which may, in the future, be demanded here, might be interesting. These remarks apply primarily to in-hand (halter) classes, but the appropriate sections may be adapted to a ridden class, and there are certain variations depending on whether the horse is shown in English or in Western tack. Whichever tack is used, it is important that it is clean and properly fitted, and that the horse is well-groomed and tidily presented.

If the horse is shown in Western tack, the mane may be hogged, but the forelock and a tuft over the withers must be left. If left free, the hair should be about 4 inches long, and lying flat on one side. In English tack, the mane may be plaited.

The tail of a Quarter Horse shown Western may be thinned and shortened to hock length or a little below; when shown English, it may be plaited, Any long hair on the jaws or legs may be clipped, and it is expected that a bridle path of between $1\frac{1}{2}$ and 6 inches should be clipped behind the ears.

There are certain conventions regarding the actual showing of Quarter Horses in the ring. Many of these will be familiar to British exhibitors, but some of the finer details are given rather more attention. For instance, when leading the horse, the rein is held in the right hand about 16–18 inches from the head-collar or halter. (If a leading rein with a chain or shank is used, the handler should hold the rein and *not* the chain.) The rest of the rein is held in the left hand, but it must not be coiled tightly or rolled up, as this is regarded as a fault. As in English classes, the horse should lead easily and willingly. The individual walk and trot are performed as in English classes, and considerably more attention is paid to turning the horse to the right, so that the handler is turning round the horse, and not the horse round the handler.

When posing the horse it must stand square, and the handler is expected to stand in front, but not directly in front of the horse, facing it. The rein remains in the right hand throughout, the remainder in the left hand, and the handler is expected to be on the opposite side of the horse's head from the judge during inspection.

At all times, the handler is required to keep the horse alert, even when the judge is inspecting another animal – judges have been known to turn round, and will not be impressed by a horse or handler that is half asleep!

The dress of the handler is considered important in Quarter Horse classes, as it is (or should be) in ordinary English in-hand classes. Neatness and tidiness make a good impression, with an emphasis on long hair (in both males and females) being tied back or concealed under a cap or hat.

PALOMINOS

Palominos are, of course, a colour not a breed, and there is some slight difference of opinion about how they should be judged – some placing more emphasis on colour than on conformation and action, others taking almost the opposite view.

The ideal colour of a Palomino should be that of a newly minted gold coin, but as this perfect shade is found in relatively few animals, three shades lighter or darker are permitted. No white is allowed on the body (saddle marks and scars are not considered as the natural colour), and dappling is not favoured by judges. If, however, the dapples are

Palomino colour in the middle and surrounded by a pattern of slightly paler hairs, this is preferred to a colouring that is almost grey all over. Dappling, when present, is nearly always in young animals and is often a sign of condition. In general, dappled animals are placed below those with whole-coloured coats. Sometimes a horse with an otherwise quite good Palomino colour has a few prominent, dark 'thumb-marks' and, as a rule, this type of marking would be preferred to an animal with sooty discoloration all down the knees and hocks, and a tail with a high proportion of grey hairs. Manes and tails must be white, not flaxen, grey or silver – but up to 15 per cent of coloured hair is permitted.

Those judges who believe that colour is slightly more important than conformation and way of going (say, in a ratio of 55:45) will probably line the class up with the horses having the best colour at the top – unless, as one judge remarked, 'one is actually deformed'. Very often the next step is to walk down the back of the line, examining the tails very carefully, as it is in these that dark hairs most often appear. Frequently there is a dark patch just over the dock. Next, the manes are inspected, including the forelock, as it is not unknown for an otherwise well-coloured horse to have a grey forelock. The judge then appraises the animals for total body colour, and clarity of mane and tail.

Having assessed the colour, the judge then looks more closely at conformation, and it is at this stage that most Palomino judges have some misgivings. Sometimes the animal with the best conformation is a bad colour. In this situation some resolve the difficulty by emphasising that in this class they are judging Palominos, and therefore the horse of good conformation but bad colour must go some way down the line as *it is not a good Palomino*. They argue that if the better-shaped horse is put up, the class might just as well be judged as bays or browns, or any other colour.

The other school of thought is perhaps less definite in its views and judgements, and makes the very difficult attempt at compromise. These judges certainly look for good colour, but to instance an extreme case, if faced with a good horse of poor colour, they might well prefer it to a poor horse of good colour, arguing that a bad horse should not win a show class. Fortunately such extremes are comparatively rare. Both schools of thought are agreed that if two horses at the top of the line are equal in make and shape, the one with the best colour must win. If these two are almost the same colour, very fine points of judging are required to make a decision. The darkness of the eyes (wall eyes are not permitted) may be considered, and in the very last resort the v-shape at the top of the tail is inspected, and the horse in which this shows the best Palomino colour will probably win. (So far as is known, it has never been necessary in this country to base a judgement on such a fine point, but it can and does happen in the United States.)

There are no foal classes for Palominos, as they are not eligible for registration, but there are other young stock classes. Judges consider these must be judged on the day, in spite of the fact that experience may suggest that an individual animal with a good colour as a yearling may change colour quite considerably at maturity. At the end of the season there is some room for variation of this general rule, with some judges preferring a rather pale yearling, provided it has a good sort of 'pinky' colour round the eyes, ears, hocks, and muzzle, as it will probably develop into a good colour by the time it is three or four years old.

Judges are, on occasion, called upon to judge part-bred Arab Palominos, and are then faced with another dilemma:

whether to put up the best part-bred Arab or the best Palomino. Opinions are again rather divided and in many ways it may be said that Palomino classes are among the most difficult to judge, and, as a consequence, some of the most unpredictable in which to compete.

APPALOOSAS

Spotted horses have been in Britain in small numbers for centuries, but it was only in 1976 that the British Appaloosa Society was formed, and produced its own standards and rules of judging. These are based on the Appaloosa Horse Club of America, and are similar to those of the Appaloosa Society of Australia – the British Society being affiliated to both.

The Appaloosa Society lays down percentage marks for the various points of judging. In the in-hand classes, 40 per cent of the marks are allocated for conformation, and 20 per cent each for type, soundness, and action. In ridden classes, 60 per cent are allocated for performance, 25 per cent for conformation and 15 per cent for turn-out.

Apart from looking for a symmetrical riding-type horse of between 14.2 and 15.3 hands (approximately), with a brisk, elastic walk, the Appaloosa judge notes the coat markings of the entries. Those eligible for registration with the British Society are as follows: *Leopard*-spotted animals – spots of any colour on a light or white background. Spots of different colours, such as black and chestnut, may be present on the same animal. *Blanket*-spotted animals – a white rump or back on which there may or may not be spots of any colour. *Snowflake*-spotted animals – white spots on any colour except grey. Some types of blue or red roan which are light on the forehead and over the loins, back and hips, but dark down the frontal bones, are also eligible. Mares are sometimes less spectacularly marked than the males.

When the horses have walked round, in an in-hand class they are lined up and examined individually. During this the judge, in addition to noting the usual points of conformation to be expected in a riding-horse, checks that the essential Appaloosa characteristics of the white sclera round the eye and the mottled skin are present in addition to the coat markings. Characteristics which *may* be present, but are not mandatory, include vertically light-and-dark-striped hoofs, and a fine-haired, whispy mane and tail.

With a picture of a quality riding-horse in mind, the judge looks for a horse with a lean head having a straight profile, wide forehead, and pointed ears of medium size. The parti-coloured skin should show clearly round the nostrils and lips, and the white sclera gives the eye prominence. The neck is expected to be a quality one, merging into a deep chest which should not be too wide, as this is considered a conformation fault. The neck should also merge into long, sloping shoulders, topped by prominent, well-defined withers. Low withers are penalised. The forearm must be strong, well muscled, long, wide and tapering down to a broad, flat, knee. Below the knee, the cannon, as would be expected in a riding-horse, must be short, flat, and wide, with no tying in. Long, sloping pasterns are preferred, and deep, open hooves, wide at the heel and with no sign of boxiness.

A short, straight back leading to strong loins is essential, and the under-line of the horse should be long, as in the Quarter Horse, and must not slope up sharply to the flanks to give a herring-gutted appearance. The judge also looks for well-rounded quarters and strong, muscular thighs and gaskins, leading to clean, wide, straight hocks. As in the foreleg, there must be no tying-in below the knee, and the hoof, while narrower than the forefoot, should have a wide heel, a large, elastic frog, strong bars and a concave sole.

Appaloosas may be shown either with a full mane or hogged, and the tail, if of the full variety, should be trimmed to fall to or just above the hocks.

Under no circumstances must conformation, action, manners or quality be sacrificed for coat colouring, but if two horses appear to be inseparable in every other way, the one with the most typical markings should be placed first.

Appaloosas tend to be of two types. In Britain so far, the hunter type is the most common, as this is the most suitable for the activities in which Appaloosas here take part. In the United States, and possibly in Australia, there is also the more compact, muscular, Quarter Horse type. Personal preference will clearly influence the judge's final decision with regard to type.

Chapter 8

THE HARNESS CLASSES

PRIVATE DRIVING

In Private Driving classes held under the auspices of the British Driving Society, the judge looks at the conformation and action of the horse or pony, the general turn-out of animal, driver and vehicle, and for an animal that is suitable for an amateur to drive. (The latter does not mean that it must necessarily be driven by an amateur.)

The classes enter at the walk and the judge gains the first impression of the turn-outs, which, as in the ridden classes, is very often a lasting impression. For instance, a good horse in a poor vehicle, or vice versa, is immediately obvious, and an untidily dressed whip will also be noted, as this too, tends to spoil the overall picture. The suitability of the horse to the vehicle is assessed. For example, a Welsh Section D cob looks correct in a gig or a float, but would be totally out of place in a Spider Phaeton, for which a hackney would be more appropriate. There is a body of opinion against a Thoroughbred-type animal in Private Driving, principally because judges feel that it just does not look right.

The walk in a harness horse is very important, and judges comment that far too many fail rather badly at this pace – showing too little length of stride, lack of impulsion and a slightly 'pottery' action. After allowing time for the class to settle, the judge asks them to trot on. In Private Driving a very extravagant action is not considered necessary, but the animal must cover the ground well. Good manners are indispensable in a horse or pony that is likely to be on busy roads, and any animal that naps, rears, takes too great a hold or is disobedient in any way will be faulted. Any animal that shows signs of collar-shyness is also penalised.

After the initial walk and trot round the ring on both reins, the class is lined up – not in any particular order – so that the judge may inspect the animals and the vehicles closely. The harness is carefully checked to see that it fits, is correctly adjusted and is clean and supple – the latter being most important in the case of the reins. Judges do not approve of over-checks in Private Driving and feel that bearing reins should not be necessary. A careful note is usually made of the bitting, as this gives some clue as to how the animal may be expected to go in the marathon phase of the class.

The vehicle itself is meticulously examined, and apart from the more obvious necessity for it to be clean and suitably painted and upholstered, it must be perfectly balanced, with the shafts level to give a level seat to the whip, and an easier, more direct pull for the horse. Small but significant points such as checking that the washers on the wheels are tight, and that the candles in the lamps have been lit at least once are not overlooked, and most judges want to see that some form of emergency equipment is carried, such as spare traces, or at the very least, a quantity of binder-twine and a knife.

Most modern vehicles are acceptable in Private Driving

classes, provided they are well made and are replicas of traditional vehicles. Modern vehicles with bicycle-type wheels are *not* favoured, chiefly because they do not flatter the horse and thus do not give the impression of a good turn-out. Show wagons are normally barred from Private Driving classes. In general, the standard of turn-out is now so high that there is little to choose between the entries at this stage, and such defects as appear are likely to be relatively minor ones.

The conformation of the horse or pony is important, but driving judges are not fanatical about this, and pay more attention to how it affects the way of going in harness than to beauty for its own sake. Nevertheless, they like to see a well-made horse or pony with some substance, and look for good head-carriage, neither too high as in some hackneys, nor too low. While a heavy or ugly head can be disguised more easily in harness (with winkers etc.), this is not a good feature, and a short neck looks even shorter with a collar on it, spoiling the balanced appearance necessary in a first-class turn-out.

Judges do not necessarily penalise a somewhat straighter shoulder or longer back than would be acceptable in a riding-horse, but a really *bad* shoulder means that the collar cannot fit correctly. A horse with a long back can be harnessed skilfully to minimise the imperfect appearance – but some judges balance this against their belief that a little extra length allows a more fluid action of the hindlegs. Faults such as tied-in elbows or bad hocks, or indeed any defect in the limbs, are unacceptable. The feet and the shoeing are usually examined with great care.

Following the inspection, each turn-out is asked to give an individual show – usually consisting of a figure of eight, a halt, and a rein-back. The judges look for smooth movement in the circles of the figure, with a slight relaxation of pace at the top of the circles, although this does not mean coming back to a walk. Animals obviously possessing a good mouth and free, flowing action are likely to be placed well. Many turn-outs are faulted on the rein-back. They either hesitate, refuse to back, or move crookedly. Failure in this is regarded extremely seriously, as in modern-day Private Driving on busy roads it is absolutely essential that all turn-outs can perform the movement correctly. Due allowance is made for the extra difficulty experienced with a four-wheeled vehicle as compared with a two-wheeled one, but even the former can be reined back straight for a few paces.

If there is time, the judge may drive all or some of the exhibits, and expects a responsive, well-mannered, pleasant drive. But as one eminent judge remarked only half jokingly, 'In the time available all you are likely to find out is that you are a better whip than the exhibitor – or, even more likely, the other way around!' Some judges like to drive the turn-outs so they can get the 'feel', and perhaps offer some advice to novices.

During the individual inspection and show, the judge also looks for unsoundness and blemishes. Curby hocks, for instance, would be held against the animal, and broken knees are regarded as a serious blemish, not only because of unsightliness, but because of the implication that the animal, having come down once, may do the same again.

Following the show-ring judging, it is customary for the competitors to go out on a marathon of approximately eight miles, during which they are observed by the judges from various points along the route. This is regarded as a helpful stage by the judges, as it is possible to see what each animal does when going up and down hill, and under normal road conditions. When the turn-out is going up hill, the judge expects that the horse will go steadily into its collar, taking the weight of the vehicle without jerks, and consistently and quietly. Downhill (which should be driven very steadily) the horse is expected to take the weight of the vehicle on the breeching, and to go smoothly and straight.

The driver is also judged, as faults sometimes creep in on a marathon that were not apparent in the ring. For example, the reins may be held in both hands instead of principally in the left, with the right just supporting; the driver may relax unduly and sit as if in a chair instead of up straight, feet braced against the footboard. The hands *should* be relaxed, thus almost guaranteeing a relaxed horse or pony.

On the return from the marathon, the final placings are made in the show-ring. The judge will assess the condition of the animal after the drive, noting if it is unduly distressed or has become over-excited. A check will be made to see if the horse or pony is wearing a different bit − changing bits for the marathon is not penalised as such, but it gives the judge some idea of the type of drive the whip had expected.

In the final analysis, having taken account of the show-ring performance, the way of going on the marathon, and the condition of the animal *after* the marathon, the judge is likely to choose the one that has gone the best and has the most impressive action, in preference to an animal with excellent conformation but an indifferent way of going.

According to the size of the show, the Private Driving classes vary in type considerably. At smaller shows there may be just the one class for all sizes and types of horses and ponies, which makes judging very difficult. At the larger shows, including the British Driving Society's Annual Show, there are separate classes for the different-sized animals, for hackney-type and non-hackney-type, and for singles, pairs, and tandems.

The Hackney-type class includes pure-bred and part-bred hackneys, and other animals that look like hackneys. It is a class to which judges may transfer horses or ponies they consider to be of hackney-type, should the necessity arise. The reason for these classes is that, while not suggesting that hackneys are invincible in driving classes, it is not very easy to judge an animal with a hackney action against others. It *can* be done, and *is* done in Championships, and in these cases the judge chooses the best Private Driving animal on the day. A show hackney might not necessarily be quite what is required of a Private Driving horse, as there are those whose spectacular action has earned them places in the show-ring, but which appear to have lost something of the ground-covering movement required for a private turn-out to be driven on the road. On the other hand, as the judges point out, hackneys are the only animals bred specifically for driving, and a really good one that moves forward well, has good conformation and perfect manners is a pleasure to see and drive – and is just as likely to win as the non-hackney type.

Judges prefer to have separate Pairs classes, because of the difficulties of making a direct comparison between them and single horses. A pair should be 'one horse twice', and although no pair ever reaches that degree of excellence, the judge looks for extremely well-matched animals with similar strides and similar action. They must pull evenly (a slack trace is a clear indication that this is lacking) and must not in any way be fighting each other. The coupling should be correct so that the horses' heads are neither too close nor too far apart, and care must be taken with the way the animals have been put to the vehicle – if the pole is too long, for example, they will be too far away from the vehicle, and the whole will appear unbalanced.

In Tandem classes, the first essential is that the horses should go straight. The leader should not be 'too much in draught', i.e. he should not be doing almost all the work. This is a common fault in tandems, often resulting in the wheeler pulling back, and a tug-of-war situation can develop. It is considered important that the leader should *be* a leader by temperament, and some judges look for considerable presence in this animal, in addition to expecting him to have good, flowing forward movement, yet be very steady at all times.

A certain amount of controversy exists about just how much the leader should do. Some judges like to see his traces taking pressure every so often, and of course he must be put into the collar going up hill or in heavy ground. Others prefer to see an almost completely slack trace. The former group criticise the latter on the grounds that a consistently slack trace looks sloppy, and more importantly, the leader cannot be put into work so quickly in an emergency. All agree, however, that the leader's trace must be slack when going downhill. It is considered to be part of the whip's skill to obtain a proper balance for the given circumstances.

The horses or ponies in a tandem need not be the same size. The wheeler would probably be more stocky and the leader lighter and a little more showy. Although a match of colour is considered attractive, this is not a very important point, and is frequently subject to changing fashions. At one time it was considered fashionable to have an odd-coloured or white leader, as it could be seen more easily in the dark, but such considerations have little relevance in modern Private Driving judging.

HACKNEYS

There are few breeds of horses or ponies possessing more presence and personality than the hackney. When a class enters the ring, these qualities are specifically sought by the judge, in addition to an overall picture of an active, well-made animal with a typically arched neck and proudly-carried head. Although the trot is, of course, the hallmark of the hackney, the judge likes to see this preceded by a brisk, active walk. The trot itself, seen from the side as the class enters the ring, must be free and flowing, balanced and light, airy, and of the truly progressive type. It should also be an even, distinct 1,2,3,4 pace, and not, as can occur in Novice classes particularly, a jerky 1, 2, 3, pause, 4. Although the trot is typically spectacular, it is not uncommon to see action which, on close observation, is of the up-and-down, pump-handle variety that does not cover the ground. This is considered faulty by the judge, who looks for the true hackney action originating from the shoulder, with very high knee action in front, followed by marked extension, with the hoof being placed lightly on the ground. A 'flip' of the hoof so that the sole is visible from the front prior to being placed on the ground is considered a fault, as is the slight pause or hesitation sometimes seen at the top of the action. The latter is often a result of trying to force the horse beyond its capabilities when schooling. The hindleg must also be raised very high with considerable extension of the hocks and pasterns, and with the hocks coming well under the horse with a crisp, piston-like precision. In the opinion of most judges, a good hackney should move 'off its hocks' perhaps more than any other breed.

The judge always asks for a change of rein, and they expect that this should be done in an orderly fashion one after the other across the diagonal, and not in the rather chaotic manner that sometimes occurs.

After the preliminary circling the class is lined up for the individual inspection and show. The judge likes to see an intelligent, courageous-looking head with a big, generous eye and alert ears. The muzzle should be neat and the nostrils large. Any coarseness of the head is regarded as a sign of bad breeding, and is penalised accordingly. A clean, well-shaped throat-latch is essential, and the head must be well set onto a long, graceful, strongly muscled neck that arches from just behind the poll and continues in the attractive curve so typical of the hackney. Ewe necks are very much disliked, not only because they look unattractive, but because they do not allow the correct head-carriage.

Sloping, riding-type shoulders are favoured, with strong muscling throughout, although the points must not be loaded. The judge looks for a strong, wide, deep chest, a good curve of ribs and barrel, a short, very strong back and loins, and long, full quarters. A well-set tail is carried artificially high, held in place by the crupper with an extension.

Good limbs are clearly important, with adequate short, flat bone in the cannons (round-bone is penalised) and sound, strong, well-shaped, straight-set feet. In front, a muscular forearm and wide, flat knees are necessary, and at the back, a strongly developed second thigh should lead to clean, well let-down hocks.

Faults sometimes seen in hackneys include short necks, too much length of back, and either long and narrow or alternatively, rather boxy feet. There is a slight tendency to be back at the knees in some animals.

When standing for inspection, hackneys normally stretch their hindlegs back somewhat, but some judges feel that the exaggerated stance sometimes seen is not necessary. It is not considered a fault, but the tendency to stand with their toes turned out seen in some hackneys is certain to invite closer examination of the legs and feet to see if it is the result of poor conformation.

After the inspection the horses are sent out for their individual show, with the judge carefully watching their action from in front and behind. Plaiting and dishing in front, and 'waving their hocks and hindfeet about' behind are the most common defects, often caused by trying to force the horse's pace beyond its natural limits. This can often lead to quite definite crossing of the forelegs as the animal tries to obtain higher knee action. Some are inclined to go with their hocks too close behind and their fetlocks and feet turned out as a result. The judge also checks that the horse holds its head straight, and not to one side as is seen from time to time.

In the final assessment of the class, both action and conformation are of great importance, although the deciding factor does vary a little from judge to judge. Some feel that rather too much emphasis is placed on action and not enough on conformation. In support of this they point out that many show hackneys are either mares, colts or stallions that may be bred from, so they should have the best possible make and shape. On the other hand, the action *is* the most distinguishing feature of a good hackney. Thus the final decision is very much a matter of personal preference.

In Novice classes the judge looks for the same conformation as in any other hackney class. Allowances are made, however, for the animals' relative lack of experience. The novice will almost certainly 'break' its stride more frequently, and either canter or simply lose its rhythm at the trot, possibly due in part to putting its feet down incorrectly. The judge bears in mind, nevertheless, that the hackney is naturally a very high-couraged animal and breaks may be due as much to over-excitement as to inexperience or faulty action. As long as the animal settles down again after a reasonable interval, it is not likely to be penalised very much in a Novice class. Novices also tire more quickly and their knee action becomes lower and lower – an aspect of the less experienced horses that is accentuated if the going is soft. In general, judges of Novice classes try to make their decisions as quickly as possible before the standard of performance begins to fall away.

On the comparatively few occasions where mares and stallions are judged together, the judge takes into account that while there may not be a great deal of difference in action, the mare will normally have slightly less front than the stallion, will not, of course, have a crest, and may be a little longer in the back.

In Pairs classes the judges look for animals that match in colour and size, and more significantly, in length of stride. In good hands a pair can be kept in perfect unison of stride for a considerable time, and this, naturally, gives the turn-out a great advantage. In novice pairs, perfect unison is obtainable less often and for shorter periods. Because of inexperience, one of the pair is inclined to lose its nerve momentarily, and a good whip will slow the pace until the two come together again.

Tandems are, in a sense, similar to pairs, but *exact* matching of size is not quite so important. If there is a slight difference, the leader must be the smaller of the two, and it is essential that it be a leader by temperament. The wheeler may be slightly heavier and possibly have a little less action. The traces of the lead horse should not be quite taut in a tandem that is going well.

There are special classes for Amateur Whips and for Lady Whips at some of the larger shows, and these are judged exactly as for any other hackney class with regard to action and conformation. Special attention will be paid to their manners and their suitability for the class, and any markedly difficult drive would be penalised.

In-hand hackney classes are judged in a similar manner to in-hand classes of other breeds, but a great deal of attention is given to balanced movement.

HACKNEY PONIES

Hackney ponies may be up to 14 hands in height, and must show genuine pony type with real pony heads, and not be miniature hackney horses. A pony with a horsy head will be placed down the line. The ponies often have the most tremendous action, and while the horses may 'float' more, the best ponies are often breathtakingly spectacular.

Chapter 9

THE ALL-ROUNDERS

WESTERN CLASSES

Western Riding classes in Britain are held under the auspices of the Western Horsemen's Association of Great Britain. There are three standard classes: Western Pleasure; Novice Western Pleasure; and Western Horsemanship. Of these, Western Horsemanship is a test of the rider's ability rather than an assessment of the conformation and action of the horse. It will therefore be mentioned only briefly for the sake of completeness. Additional classes include Trail Horse, Western Stock, Reining, Versatility, and Western Riding, and as all these involve judging of the horse itself – either its paces, or conformation, or both – they will be discussed in more detail.

WESTERN PLEASURE

This class is the nearest Western equivalent of the English Hack or Riding-horse class, with 60 per cent of the marks allocated for performance, 15 per cent for conformation, and 25 per cent for the neatness of horse and rider.

The Western Horsemen's Association has laid down specific rules for dress, tack, and the points to be judged. Riders must, of course, be in Western dress, including a felt or straw Western hat, Western trousers or jeans and a plain or coloured shirt, with the sleeves buttoned down. Any type of Western tie must be worn. The following items *may* be worn but are not mandatory: a jacket or waistcoat, Western boots, chaps and gloves. A lariat may be carried; spurs may be worn, but the judge penalises any misuse of these very heavily. Riders are not permitted to carry crops or quirts. The turn-out of riders in Western classes in Britain has been controversial, and great efforts are being made to raise the standard. The days when guns and sheriff's badges appeared with monotonous regularity are *almost* gone, but most judges agree that there is still room for improvement. As much care should be taken with Western turn-out as in an English hack or hunter class, and there is room for neat and carefully co-ordinated colour schemes to complement the horse's colour. Judges are not yet expecting the extreme attention that is paid to turn-out in Western classes in America, but the standard is rising all the time.

The horse must have a Western saddle with a saddle blanket. Although some elaborate, highly decorative saddles are used, these will not gain more marks than the ordinary, well-made working saddle. Any type of Western bridle or hackamore is to be used, with a humane Western bit. Although it is not mandatory, some judges expect any animal over five years of age to be wearing a bit and accepting it correctly. Martingales or tie-downs are banned, as are curb chains or rawhide curb straps under the chin. Curb straps must be of leather and at least half an inch wide. Split reins are mandatory, unless hackamore, roping or California reins are used. A breast-collar is optional. Account is taken of the general cleanliness and correct fitting of the tack.

A Western Pleasure class is often judged 'on the rope', i.e. competitors are not asked to give an individual show, but this varies from judge to judge.

When the class comes in at the walk, the judge looks for a horse that is relaxed and willing, not lazy or sluggish. Most judges allow the class to walk round the ring several times to get settled, and during this time the horse's general suitability is assessed. In a Western Pleasure class the accent is on the word 'pleasure', and the judge looks for a horse that appears to be giving a comfortable, enjoyable ride by his way of going and his manners. A free, elastic, swinging and active stride is sought, which would be a pleasure to sit over long distances, but without necessarily being fast. This is sometimes called a 'flat-foot' walk, and is not quite the collected pace that is seen, for example, in an English Hack or Hunter class. The horse must, however, bring his hindlegs well under him and not be long and 'strung-out' in appearance.

The type of horse is important, and although no one breed of horse has a monopoly on Western Pleasure classes in Britain, the judges look for certain features that they consider make a good pleasure horse. A well-balanced horse with a reasonably long neck and good shoulder, so there is plenty in front of the rider, is required, with a good head-carriage. The rather high head-carriage of the Arab is not considered suitable by some judges, though others would disagree. Strong limbs and good quarters are essential, and the animals must present an attractive picture overall. The ideal maximum size is about 15.2 hands, otherwise mounting and dismounting may be difficult. A very large, heavy, hunter-type horse would not normally be the choice for high placing in a Pleasure Horse class, but it will depend very much on the standard of the other entries in the class.

Having gained first impressions, the judge asks the class to jog on – the Western equivalent of the trot. In this pace the judge looks for a very slow, smooth, contained movement, with little bounce in the stride (in contrast to the English trot) so that the rider can sit down deeply and comfortably to it (Western riders do not normally post when jogging). The horse with the long, smooth stride has a definite advantage over the animal that is only *just* trotting in an effort to maintain smoothness.

After the jog comes the lope – a very slow canter that covers the ground. It is essential that the lope is not hurried or bouncy, as this would not be comfortable over long distances. A common fault in the lope is for the horses to move in four-time instead of three-time, probably caused by premature containment of the movement in an attempt to obtain a slower pace. The class may be asked to lope on, and although this is sometimes known as a hand gallop, it resembles an extended canter, and must remain smooth throughout.

At all paces, the judge looks for the Western Pleasure horse to be ridden on a *loose* rein contact, with the application of rein-aids only when the horse is being asked for transitions or change of direction. English riders find this extremely light contact very difficult to achieve, and the judges comment that there is, with few exceptions, far too much tension and too much rein used. Neck reining is obligatory, and the reins must be held in one hand only, with no changing over during the class. The free hand should rest on the rider's thigh and not on the saddle, but holding the reins with the free hand, about 16–20 inches from the reining hand is permitted. One judge observed that the free hand often indicates tension in the rider, and consequently in the horse. The rider should maintain a relaxed position in the saddle, but without slouching, and should look comfortable and as if the ride is a pleasure.

Throughout the class the horse must maintain the required pace until asked to do otherwise; it must be obedient in all ways, perform well on both reins, and go on the correct lead. A horse that needs to be kicked on or spurred unduly will not be placed well.

Having seen the horses perform all the paces on both reins, the judge will line the class up, and almost certainly ask each competitor to rein back individually to show the horse's obedience and suppleness. The same points are noted as in any rein-back, with tossing of the head, opening of the mouth and crooked movement all being penalised.

If an individual show is required, it may either be one of the rider's own choice, or the judge may direct each competitor to perform a set series of movements. Either method can be very revealing, with a horse that has gone well until this stage suddenly 'blowing up' or napping, or performing the test inadequately. Most tests include a figure of eight with a simple change, with the judge taking special note that the horse changes both in front and behind. Some judges may ask for an about-turn, consisting of coming down from a lope to a jog to a walk, followed by a neat, square halt and a smooth turn before proceeding in the opposite direction.

NOVICE WESTERN PLEASURE

This class is judged as for the Open Western Pleasure, but entries are restricted to horses or ponies that have not won a first or second prize. Three-year-olds (which may be shown after July 1st in their three-year-old year) are an exception – they remain novices for that year, irrespective of any awards. They must be shown in either a bosal, or an English or Western snaffle, or any humane Western bit.

Clearly, in a Novice class of this type, a wide range of age and ability may be encountered. A number of horses will be much greener, probably a bit on their forehands, and less steady than in an Open class, but the judge looks for the same points of conformation, action and turn-out, while making allowance for the fact that they are judging novices. Most prefer to put up a promising youngster above what is sometimes called 'a perpetual novice' – a horse that is never going to be good enough to win or be placed second.

WESTERN STOCK CLASS

This class is designed to demonstrate that a horse has the ability to perform certain movements and tasks that would be required when working cattle. The dress and tack are the same as for the Western Pleasure class, with the addition of a lariat, and, if closed reins are used, hobbles.

The marks for judging differ slightly, with 75 per cent for performance, 15 per cent for conformation, and 10 per cent for turn-out.

The class comes into the ring as a Pleasure class and the horses are judged on their paces in a similar fashion. However the judge is probably looking for a rather different type of horse. A heavier, much more muscled-up horse that is suitable for stock work is required – typically a Quarter Horse or a Quarter Horse cross, that is heavy and strong enough to hold a roped steer.

The paces having been judged, the class will either leave the ring or be lined up at one end, while each competitor performs a set of prescribed movements, designed to show the horse's suppleness, agility, obedience and general suit-

ability for cattle work. The test normally consists of six
phases:

Quick start and sliding stop
Settle horse for ten seconds, then back up
Small figure of eight, slowly
Large figure of eight, fast
Ground-tie (or hobble if closed reins are used)
Rope test

In the quick start and sliding stop, the judges expect to
see a horse move from a standstill or perhaps a jog into a
gallop. The extent of the gallop will obviously depend on
the size of the ring, but from it the horse must perform a
controlled sliding stop. In this the animal halts in a very
short distance, sliding his hindquarters right underneath
him and bringing his forefeet off the ground. Common
faults in this quite difficult movement include the horse
being uncollected and too much on the forehand, so that it
is impossible to get the quarters underneath. The animal
then 'props' to a stiff, ungainly standstill, with the rider out
of the saddle instead of sitting down in it. A horse that
grinds to a halt with an open mouth and head thrown up
will be penalised. Quite often in Britain the going is too slip-
pery for sliding stops to be performed; some judges consider
that any grass surface is unsuitable, and will only ask for
this manoeuvre to be performed if a dirt arena or an indoor
school is being used. Where a sliding stop is not practicable,
the judge may ask for a good firm halt from a jog. Assuming
that the halt (of whichever variety) has been performed,
the horse is then settled for 10 seconds, and backed up
(reined back) for several strides. As in any rein-back, the
judge expects to see decisive, straight movement, with no
evasions or head tossing.

The small figure of eight should be executed at a slow lope. Whether the horse does a simple or a flying change in the middle is usually left to the rider's discretion (and ability!) but whichever is performed, the judge looks for a correct lead and a change behind as well as in front. Failure to do this is quite common, particularly in a flying change, and loses many marks.

The large figure of eight is performed in a similar manner, but at a fast lope.

After the figures of eight, the rider dismounts for the ground-tying. In this, the open reins are left to touch the ground, and the rider walks some distance away from the horse, which should remain stationary with its head up. Faults in this are obvious, and include the rider not walking a sufficient distance from the horse, the horse moving from the position in which it was placed, or putting its head down to graze.

The final phase is the rope test. There is more than one way of performing this. In the first, the rider throws his rope, and this should be the signal for the horse to stop. Having secured the rope to the saddle horn, the rider dismounts and runs to the far end of the rope and picks it up. A well-trained horse then takes up the slack and pulls against it, as if there was a calf on the end. Alternatively, a ring steward attaches the rope, when thrown, to a log or other heavy object. The rider does not have to dismount, and the horse should back up, pulling the log on the end of the rope. Throughout, the judge looks for a well-balanced, obedient horse that performs smoothly in all phases. Uneven, choppy paces are faulted, as these are tiring and unsuitable in an animal that might be asked to work cattle for many hours in the course of a day.

REINING CLASS

The Reining class may be described as the Western equivalent of the dressage test, in that the horse and rider are required to perform a series of set movements (known as a Reining Pattern) in an arena measuring about 50 × 150 ft, containing various markers. The judging is of performance by both rider and horse.

The tests used by the Western Horsemen's Association are similar to those of the American Quarter Horse Association, and are performed at a fast lope unless otherwise stated. The dress and tack are as for Western Pleasure classes, except that curb chains are allowed; these must be at least half an inch wide, lie flat against the jaw and be approved by the judge.

The tests include sliding stops, back-ups, small and large figures of eight, pivots, and roll-backs over the hocks. The last two may be unfamiliar to British spectators, at least under those names. A pivot is virtually a turn on the haunches, with the hindlegs acting as a pivot point around which the forelegs move. In the Reining Pattern, pivots are a relatively slow movement, through 90 or 180 degrees. Roll-backs over the hocks are much more spectacular, and consist of a complete about-turn at speed, with the horse getting its hocks right under it and pivoting on the hindlegs, before moving quickly off in the opposite direction. Both the pivot and the roll-back must be performed very smoothly, with the rider sitting well down in the saddle.

Throughout the Reining Pattern, the judge looks for a smooth, resistance-free performance from the horse. Penalties are incurred for anticipation of commands, head tossing, over-excitement, or (as the Americans so aptly describe it) tail wringing. Dropping from a lope into a jog is also penalised. The rider incurs penalties for errors of course:

knocking over markers, changing the rein hand or using two hands, losing a stirrup, holding onto the saddle, excessive spurring or use of the whip, and jerking of reins.

TRAIL HORSE CLASS

The Trail Horse class is not far removed from the English Handy Hunter or Handy Pony class, with entries being judged on the three basic paces and on their ability to negotiate a series of obstacles or hazards. Performance is allocated 75 per cent of the marks, and condition and neatness of horse and rider 25 per cent. (The official phrasing is slightly ambiguous, but it may be taken that 'condition' refers to the horse!)

The tack is as for Western Pleasure classes, but in addition a lariat or slicker (raincoat) must be carried on the saddle.

Normally six or eight of the following obstacles must be negotiated: opening, passing through, and closing a gate; passing over a bridge; dragging a log backwards and forwards using a rope round the saddlehorn; stepping over or between several logs or tyres; picking up and carrying a sack of cans whilst mounted; a small jump, not exceeding 2 ft in height; dismounting and leading the horse over the jump; backing along a safe, indicated L-shaped corridor composed of logs; mounting and dismounting from both sides; donning or removing the slicker whilst mounted; permitting a second rider to mount and riding double; groundtying (hobbling) the horse (hobbling is called for where closed reins or bosal are in use); loading the horse into a trailer; negotiating a water hazard; leading a spare horse.

Judging is similar to that of a Handy Hunter class in English shows, with handiness, agility and smoothness of performance taken into account — but timing is not a factor. In this class the reining hand may be changed when negotiating an obstacle.

VERSATILITY CLASS

This, as the name perhaps suggests, is judged on the horses' ability to perform well under both Western and English tack. Performance is allocated 60 per cent of the marks, conformation 15 per cent, and neatness of horse and rider, 25 per cent.

Entries are judged first as for a Western Pleasure class, but may be required to perform a pivot. A quick change is then made into English tack, and the horse is judged at the walk, trot and canter; it may be asked to jump a small fence of minimum height 2 ft 6 in. and maximum 3 ft.

The rider must be appropriately dressed for each section, but jodphurs and English boots are permitted under Western chaps, and Western shirts under English jackets.

In addition to judging the basic paces, the judge is likely to favour those horses that are able to make a definite distinction in their way of going for the two sections. For example, a horse that is able to show some real extension in his paces in the English section will probably be preferred to a horse whose paces show no appreciable difference.

With regard to conformation, there is no set type, but the judge looks for an attractive horse that appears to be a pleasant ride under both saddles, and with no very obvious faults.

WESTERN RIDING CLASS

This class is designed to test the merits of a 'sensible, well-mannered, free-and-easy moving ranch horse which can get its rider around on the usual ranch course over the trails, or give a quiet, comfortable and pleasant ride in open country, through and over obstacles.' Competitors are required to perform a set Western Riding Pattern, which includes sections to be ridden at the walk, jog and lope respectively, the negotiation of a gate, and passing over a log that is just large enough to break the horse's stride. The Pattern also includes changes of direction, loping through a line of markers, and loping a figure that resembles an angular serpentine.

The horses are judged on their paces, the correct change of leads, manners, temperament, response to their rider, and overall smoothness and correctness of performance.

WESTERN HORSEMANSHIP

This is similar to an English Best Rider class, and is judged on the rider's ability to demonstrate the various Western paces. The conformation of the horse is not judged.

RIDING-HORSES

Riding-horse classes are held at many shows up and down the country, and there is a huge variation in the type and standard of entry – depending to some extent on the size and standing of the show. At the larger shows, the Riding-horse class may be affiliated to the British Show Hack and Cob Association, and judged under the Association's rules by an official judge. These classes are likely to attract some very high-quality animals. At smaller shows, the standard may also be good at the top end of the line, but there will more likely be a proportion of entries that are not really up to show standard, but whose owners want to 'have a go' and obtain some experience of the show-ring. Judging at small shows may be more variable, sometimes because the schedule does not lay down any hard-and-fast rules or guidelines for either judges or competitors. They are, nonetheless, very popular classes, and serve a most useful purpose as an introduction to showing.

In classes held under British Show Hack and Cob Association rules, the judges are given some guidance. The horse must be over 14.2 hands, and show some substance and quality; it must be capable of performing the same movements as required in a hack. In some classes, entries must jump two small, natural fences (not exceeding 3 ft 6 in.) as part of their individual show. Marks are awarded as follows: 40 per cent for conformation, presence and true action; 20 per cent each for ride, manners and training, and jumping performance. Horses are eliminated in the jumping phase for three refusals, and thus lose 20 per cent of the total marks. In classes omitting the jumping phase, 40 per cent is allotted to conformation, presence and true action, and 60 per cent for ride, manners and training.

Riding-horse classes are not easy to judge, because there is often such a variety among the entry – hack-types, hunter-types, cob-types, Arabs, Thoroughbreds, lightweights, heavyweights – the possibilities are endless. Some shows attempt to ease the difficulties by dividing the horses into two classes: usually for those up to and including 15.3 hands, and those over 15.3.

In general, judges do not want quite so much quality and elegance in a riding-horse as in a hack, nor as much size and substance as in a heavyweight hunter, but if either of these, or a really good cob, went superbly well, they could be well placed. They tend to look more for an all-purpose animal, with some quality, excellent limbs, sound overall conformation, a kindly temperament and good manners.

The individual show should include a figure of eight, halt, and rein-back – all performed neatly and correctly –

and in a class where jumping is required, the judge looks for a horse that takes the fences smoothly and sensibly, neither rushing into them nor requiring a great deal of pushing. A riding-horse may be asked to gallop, and should show a free-moving but controlled pace, and pull up smoothly and willingly. One description of a riding-horse that perhaps sums up the judges' requirements rather well is: 'An attractive-looking horse that the rider can have lots of fun with, capable of doing a bit of hacking and a bit of jumping, without necessarily being expected to win a purely show class at a big show.'

At the smaller shows it is almost impossible to give very much indication of the type of animal required, as there are almost as many opinions as there are judges. Acceptable conformation, manners and good movement will be taken into account, but beyond that, personal likes and dislikes will almost certainly be the deciding factor.

FAMILY PONIES

Family-pony classes are rather similar to Riding-horse classes in that the judge is likely to be faced with a wide variety of animals. The similarity, however, more or less ends there, because the Family-pony judge will almost certainly take general suitability into account more than faultless conformation and action. Opinions vary about the ideal Family pony, but most judges agree that they are looking for an animal that can safely be ridden and enjoyed by a young child (of about eight years of age, for instance) and all ages in between up to a moderately lightweight parent. To expect a pony to be suitable for a small child *and* a heavy man is probably asking too much.

The ideal size is likely to be about 14 hands – 14.2 is a

little too tall for the younger child – and thus a native pony that can carry more weight for its size than most others is likely to be favoured. Width (or narrowness) is obviously important, so that the cobby-type of half-bred pony, or one with, for example, Irish draught blood, is probably less suitable.

The judge will almost certainly pay close attention to the pony's length of stride. In this, the larger members of the family may have to suffer a little for the smaller, and have a shorter-striding animal than makes for real comfort. It is virtually impossible for a small child to have any sort of control over a pony while he or she is suspended in mid-air, trying to rise to a long-striding trot.

A small head and a moderately short neck (even if the head is slightly out of proportion to the rest of the body) can be an advantage, because it will be 'self-carrying'. It will also tend to be carried quite high, and the smaller-headed, shorter-necked pony does, in any event, incline to a shorter stride.

The judges will try and assess the pony's temperament as this is of great importance for a number of reasons. Firstly, it must not be stubborn – a small child on a 14-hand pony has little chance of overcoming any resistance, chiefly because its legs can only reach a short distance down the pony's side. The pony must be sensible, amiable and placid enough to accept that the leg aids, for instance, are going to vary widely according to which member of the family is riding. In this respect, a young pony is not particularly suitable – having only been broken and schooled comparatively recently, it is much more likely to become confused and upset by aids being applied in different places. A pony that responds to the voice has a great deal in its favour.

Although it is not easy to assess in the ring, a Family

pony must be sure-footed – the younger member of the family is unlikely to have the strength to hold it together – and in any event, it can be quite alarming for a small child to be on a 14-hand animal that stumbles.

Some judges attach significance to colour. The Family pony will be expected to go out at all times in all weathers during school holidays, and black and chestnut ponies, being thinner skinned, are going to be much more distressed by flies than, for example, a bay or a grey. A black pony is also going to suffer more in hot weather.

Arguably, preference may be given to geldings rather than mares. This obviates the problem of mares being in season at the very time the children want to go to shows and gymkhanas, and, on the whole, geldings are temperamentally steadier, and less likely to be kickers.

As can be seen, conformation as such has played a much less important role than in the usual show classes. Nevertheless it must be taken into consideration to some extent, if only because a badly-made pony is also likely to be a very uncomfortable one, and will not give the pleasure that should be expected from the ideal Family pony.

RIDE AND DRIVE

The Ride and Drive classes of the British Driving Society are not the same as those seen on television, which are judged on time through a set course of obstacles, with penalties for errors of course and knock-downs. In these classes the conformation and action of the animals are not judged.

The British Driving Society Ride and Drive classes are regarded as show classes, with the horses and ponies being judged in two phases, as the name indicates. The method of final placings recommended is to place each entry as a driving-horse or driving-pony, then as a riding-horse or riding-pony, and finally to add the two placings together, with the animal having the lowest total marks winning. For example, an animal placed second in the riding section and fourth in the driving – making a total of six – will be placed below one placed second in the riding and third in the driving – making a total of five. In the event of equality of marks, the one with the highest placing in the driving section is the winner. In common with other marking systems, this *can* lead to not wholly satisfactory results, and it has been known for an animal that is a reasonable ride and very bad drive to obtain better placing than one that is a good drive.

The driving section is judged as in a normal Private Driving class. In the riding section, the judge looks for a well-balanced animal with a good head-carriage, that moves freely with its hocks well underneath. The animal should show a good rhythm in walk, trot and canter, with smooth transitions up and down, and be able to perform a figure of eight with a simple change. The horse or pony must be well mannered at all times.

Penalties will be incurred for lack of balance and free forward movement, leading with the wrong leg, poor or indifferent transitions, and any other faults which make a horse or pony uncomfortable or unpleasant to ride, such as pulling or refusing to accept the bridle.

INDEX